NAVIGATING LIFE

Andrew Phang

NAVIGATING LIFE

Reflections and Stories

Illustrations by Christine Phang

Published in 2023 by Marshall Cavendish Editions
An imprint of Marshall Cavendish International

All rights reserved

The publisher makes no representation or warranties with respect to the contents of
this book, and specifically disclaims any implied warranties or merchantability or
fitness for any particular purpose, and shall in no event be liable for any loss of profit
or any other commercial damage, including but not limited to special, incidental,
consequential, or other damages.

Other Marshall Cavendish Offices:
Marshall Cavendish Corporation, 800 Westchester Ave, Suite N-641, Rye Brook,
NY 10573, USA • Marshall Cavendish International (Thailand) Co Ltd, 253 Asoke,
16th Floor, Sukhumvit 21 Road, Klongtoey Nua, Wattana, Bangkok 10110, Thailand
• Marshall Cavendish (Malaysia) Sdn Bhd, Times Subang, Lot 46, Subang Hi-Tech
Industrial Park, Batu Tiga, 40000 Shah Alam, Selangor Darul Ehsan, Malaysia

Marshall Cavendish is a registered trademark of Times Publishing Limited

National Library Board, Singapore Cataloguing in Publication Data

Name(s): Phang, Andrew Boon Leong. | Phang, Christine, illustrator.
Title: Navigating life : reflections and stories / Andrew Phang ; illustrations by
Christine Phang.
Description: Singapore : Marshall Cavendish Editions, 2023.
Identifier(s): ISBN 978-981-5084-15-3 (paperback)
Subject(s): LCSH: Conduct of life. | Success. | Interpersonal relations.
Classification: DDC 158.1--dc23

Printed in Singapore

Cover art and illustrations by Christine Phang

To the Memory of My Parents,

Mr Phang Sing Eng and Mrs Peggy Phang

CONTENTS

Work, Service and Rest

Finding Meaning in Life

Reflections on Life in a Time of Pandemic

Preface

As a lecturer, I found it especially enriching to talk not only about the law but also about life (and, in return, to hear from my students about both, especially the latter). Indeed, to a large extent, the law is about life – although, of course, life is much more than the law. And in talking about life, I often found it most impactful when I shared from my own life or from the lives of others. I was, essentially, telling stories. And I found that they were more effective than I could have imagined. Stories help those listening to remember far more effectively. And in remembering, I believe that they draw upon the lessons embedded within each story and are more likely to apply them to their own lives. There is also a sense of realism. Many life lessons are often conveyed in the abstract and hence perceived to be dry, arid and didactic, with no direct practical application as such.

Back in my youth, my mother was the most effective teacher I knew. She taught chemistry but her students remembered her even after they had left the subject behind them. Many would go on to be leaders in diverse fields. She also taught her children well – principally in the form of life lessons. She would illustrate them by reference to our everyday experiences and we could therefore relate to them and also remember the lessons taught. For example, she taught us never to use others and then discard them. She likened this to squeezing juice from sugar cane (a popular local drink). I could relate to that right away because, although I enjoyed the drink very much, I also recalled how the vendor would push the cut sections of sugar cane stems through the machine to be pressed, and the extruded remnants were pretty awful to look at and would be discarded in wicker baskets behind the stall. I mention this particular story for two reasons. The first is that I have never forgotten that lesson and have always endeavoured not to use others but to encourage and uplift them whenever possible. The second is that I began to relate this story on occasion, at the commencement of each court term, to the Justices' Law Clerks (who are drawn from the top law graduates in both local and overseas law schools). This story has apparently been passed down from one generation of law clerks to another (even when I have not personally related it to a particular cohort).

One day, it occurred to me that these life lessons were more valuable than even the latest legal principles. After all, the law keeps changing and one has to keep up with the changes. However, these life principles are universal and unchanging in nature. More importantly, they are also indispensable to life – and living a meaningful life. And I therefore began to record these life lessons, commencing with the above "No Crushed Sugar Cane" story. In addition to my mother's life stories, I began to realise how, by his conduct (in particular, his self-sacrificial love), my father also "wrote" stories – not in a conventional sense but, just as importantly, by living his life as he did. As I continued to record these stories, I began to realise that, having now lived well over six decades, I had life stories to tell as well. I must confess that I was quite surprised initially. I am not a dynamic person; on the contrary, I am a very quiet person and very private by nature, although I come out of my shell when I feel very strongly about something and/or have a mission to accomplish (such as teaching my students).

I also realised that we *all* have life stories that might be of interest to others, if nothing else, because we are all so different.

What we might consider routine and mundane might not be considered as such by others, especially if they can draw life lessons from our stories. I therefore added my own stories as well as experiences. I have often wondered why we do not often share from our own lives. I think that this is because of fear. However, a lesson learnt that can be conveyed is always useful and we should never be embarrassed to share from our lives (even if, perhaps especially if, it does not put us in particularly good light). If others would think less of us as a result, then, in my view at least, that is their problem, not mine. Indeed, from my own experience, I have learnt that authenticity is especially valued – perhaps because it is becoming increasingly rare in a world where weakness is frowned upon and material success highly valued.

What you have in this slim collection is a distillation of my own experiences on life and the nuggets of wisdom which have guided me in my life's journey – hence the title of this book, *Navigating Life*. As already mentioned, it comprises reflections, many of which are in the form of stories, hence the sub-title, *Reflections and Stories*. It is a slim volume because, quite frankly, there are only a few truly essential or core principles to living a meaningful life. The reader will also notice a pithy summary right at the end of each reflection. This was quite essential, as it turned out, because if I could not summarise the core thought or lesson to be drawn from the reflection concerned, it might mean that the life lesson might not be appropriate or might not have been expressed clearly enough. I should add that these reflections were written over a period of several years. I did not write for the sake of writing but only set out my thoughts when I felt inspired and guided to do so. As life is "messy", there are inevitable overlaps between some reflections and I have therefore endeavoured to indicate this by cross-referencing them where appropriate.

I have written and edited many professional law books. However, this slim volume may well be the most important book I have ever written. As I have alluded to above, getting our life principles in order and then applying them are far more important than anything else. They are the foundations upon which our lives – both personal and professional – are built. I hope that you will find these reflections of interest and, most importantly, of at least potential reflection or even application in your own life.

As evident from the dedication of this book as well as the first few reflections, this book was inspired by my parents, who imparted to me the values that are reflected in this book. I would not be the person I am today without their love, guidance and sacrifice. I would also like to thank my wife, Sock Yong, for always inspiring me to be a better husband, father and person, and my daughters, Rachel and Christine, for their love which brightens my every day. All of them read the various reflections and gave me much valuable feedback. Christine, an accomplished artist, provided the beautiful illustrations in this book while Rachel, a far more accomplished wordsmith than I, provided valuable feedback on the text of the reflections themselves. In addition to reviewing the text, Sock Yong was inspirational in constantly encouraging me in my journey to complete this book and was instrumental in pointing out important values that were required to be considered. Professor (now Judicial Commissioner) Goh Yihan also provided much valuable feedback in helping me to fine-tune the categories under which the reflections were placed.

There are also many others who provided me with much appreciated feedback and assistance. In particular, I would like to thank Ms Carol Yap who assisted me in the preparation as well as formatting of the text in her spare time. I would also like to express my deep gratitude to Mr Melvin Neo for his vision, insight and encouragement, as well as to Ms Anita Teo for her able editing which made this book much better than it would otherwise have been. Above all, despite the fact that this book is intended to be accessible to everyone, regardless of belief or worldview, I cannot end without acknowledging the divine guidance which I have felt throughout from the Lord, who not only provided the inspiration but also the wisdom and strength to complete this work.

Andrew Phang
March 2023

RELATIONSHIPS

1

No Crushed Sugar Cane
How to Treat Others

My mother was an excellent teacher (and, subsequently, school principal). This was due mainly to her wonderful ability as a communicator. As a mother, she was concerned with values. This has influenced me deeply. As the years went by, I became increasingly convinced that without a strong value system, one cannot live a life that is truly meaningful. One way my mother would communicate values to us was through stories – which often (as in this reflection) constituted "word pictures" and which were all the more vivid and memorable as a result. I think that stories are powerful teaching tools, especially about life. People tend to remember stories as opposed to arid, technical facts. Stories also furnish the opportunities to convey values "in action", as it were. It is true that each person's experience is different. However, one person's experience may still be valuable insofar as it contains a kernel of wisdom, the value of which is demonstrated in the life of the person concerned. At the very least, it might provide encouragement to those who hear the story.

One such story which has been indelibly etched in my memory is that of sugar cane – or, more accurately, crushed sugar cane. Sugar cane juice is a common drink in Singapore. When I was young, I would sometimes watch these vendors (often by the roadside,

occasionally in coffee shops) pushing cut sugar cane stems through a machine. The stems would be crushed as they were run through the machine, with delicious sugar cane juice flowing down into a container below. These stems were passed repeatedly through the machine until they were crushed utterly flat. I was always fascinated by how the vendor would almost invariably take these flattened pieces of sugar cane – already long devoid of any juice – and pour some water over them before running them through the machine one last time. This was, presumably, to extract the very last drops of sugar cane juice possible. And then the inevitable next action – casting the now really pathetic-looking pieces of crushed sugar cane into a wicker basket which, when full, would be emptied and its contents ultimately carted away to the rubbish dump.

My mother constantly cautioned us *not to treat people like crushed sugar cane*. More specifically, she would tell us that we ought not to use people and then cast them away when they were no longer of any personal use to us. She would advise us not to squeeze personal benefits from people like juice from the sugar cane stem but should always be polite and respectful to all, regardless of who they are. Some might cite the view of Immanuel Kant that we should treat people as ends and not as means. Others might speak of the Golden Rule that we should do unto others what we would like others to do unto us. However, to a young Singaporean boy who enjoyed sugar cane juice, my mother's imagery was a far more effective way of conveying the same message.

There is another – and closely related – lesson. Just as I enjoy sugar cane juice, I have also learnt to be appreciative of people – in particular, the kindness and assistance that they render to me. Such kindness and assistance entails effort and (on occasion) even "crushing" effort. Many of us tend to take kindness for granted; some are even worse – they take kindness as a sign of weakness. In my view, this is unacceptable. As I have just mentioned, the complete opposite should be the case. We should all learn to appreciate people more – particularly those who help us and are kind to us.

I would just like to conclude by observing that, decades later, when I became a Christian, I found that this was how the Christian faith required me to act as well. You see, it is a natural human trait in most people to be selfish, resulting in a tendency to make use of others like crushed sugar cane. This is an imperfect world. Indeed, I must confess that I found it very difficult to conduct myself selflessly. However, after becoming a Christian, it became a little easier as I could draw on the wisdom and guidance of God. This is not to say that I became a much better person. But what I will say is that it made it a lot easier not to treat people as crushed sugar cane and, on the contrary, enabled me to be more appreciative of others and not take them for granted.

*Do not treat people like crushed
sugar cane, using them and then casting
them aside. Learn, instead,
to appreciate them more.*

2

Maintaining Appropriate Boundaries
Being Treated by Others

In many ways, the present reflection is the *converse* of the preceding one (which dealt with how we ought to treat others). It will be recalled that the previous reflection emphasised that we must not treat people like crushed sugar cane, using them and then casting them aside, and that we should learn, instead, to appreciate them more. However, what if the situation is such that *we*, in fact, are the ones being treated like crushed sugar cane? This is often the case where the person concerned is too soft and tends to say "Yes" to every request, or even direction, made to him or her. This may well lead – in substance, if not also form – to such a person being bullied and being generally taken advantage of. There is yet another situation where a person is not consciously taking advantage of another person, nevertheless the latter is what we would today term a "people pleaser" – for whatever reason, the person concerned feels that he or she can be appreciated *only* by pleasing others all the time.

I would suggest that neither of the situations I have just described is healthy. In the first situation, one merely ends up becoming a victim who is bullied and taken advantage of by others. The fact of the matter is that, regardless of our station in life, we are all unique individuals who should therefore be entitled to a minimum amount of respect and consideration. The result is that, as emphasised in the preceding reflection, others should treat us with appreciation as well as consideration.

In the second situation, the "people pleaser" is, unfortunately, acting under a misapprehension or even delusion. It is precisely because (as I have just mentioned) we are all unique individuals that none of us needs to please others in order to affirm the unique identity that is already ours. Yes, we should always be considerate and kind, and seek to help others who are truly in need. However, there is no need to go overboard merely because we feel that if we do not do so, people will think any less of us. If indeed that is the case, then such persons are not – if I may put it bluntly – worthy of respect in the first place.

In both situations, the correct – as well as balanced – approach is *the need (as well as the wisdom to know where and when) to draw the line – in other words, to maintain appropriate boundaries*. This should be the case for all aspects of our lives, whether at the workplace or in the domestic or family sphere. What the appropriate boundary is in any given situation will, of course, depend on the precise circumstances. There is perhaps no better teacher in this regard than experience, for even negative experiences can be valuable as they teach us to act in the opposite manner the next time a similar situation arises. Perhaps one valuable guideline is the converse of that stated in the previous reflection – that *we should draw the line when others seek to treat us like crushed sugar cane, that is to say, when they are seeking merely to use us and then cast us aside.* Perhaps better still, we should learn through experience to *wisely anticipate* situations when other persons may well use us like crushed sugar cane. An obvious instance is when someone has conducted himself or herself in such an inappropriate manner in the past. In fairness, we should always keep an open mind but I would respectfully suggest that we should be wary of such persons if they have, in fact, treated us like crushed sugar cane in the past.

In addition, so long as we treat others with consideration and respect, and help them if such help is indeed so required (again, the converse of treating others like crushed sugar cane), we should not overdo things and become "people pleasers" simply in order to affirm our own identities which in fact *already* belong uniquely to us.

We should maintain the appropriate boundaries, and not let others take unfair advantage of us. Neither should we be "people pleasers" and, in this regard, should also maintain appropriate boundaries with regard to how much help we render to others.

3

A 'Royal' Sacrifice, A Priceless Love
True Romantic Love

It is an understatement to observe that we live in different times. It is true that, in some ways, life has improved greatly. This is to be found mainly in the *physical* amenities we now have compared to yesteryear. In Singapore, housing used to be very rough and, on occasion, did not provide total shelter from the elements and, even when they did, they were by no means comfortable surroundings compared to the housing we live in today. There is now modern sanitation and the children of today would be shocked if they are told that, once upon a time, buckets of human waste had to be collected each day from a great many households which were bereft of modern sanitation.

However, it is also true that life has also taken a step backwards, so to speak. This is not as noticeable because it impacts largely in the sphere of the *intangible*. It is most noticeable, in my view, in the sphere of *relationships*. In particular, *true* romantic love appears to be less common than it was in the past. Although it is true that arranged marriages were common in the years gone by, it is also true that many of those marriages were quite stable and even embodied much love (even taking into account long-suffering wives who may have stayed on in a loveless marriage for the sake of survival and/or their children). What *is* clear today, however, is

that casual liaisons are quite common and single-parent families are not that uncommon nowadays. It is also clear that the divorce rate has risen significantly – and is rising. It seems to me that if a marriage begins with what I have termed *true* romance, it is more likely to be able to withstand the inevitable storms that afflict all relationships in a fundamentally imperfect as well as broken world.

I have begun with this rather lengthy preamble of sorts because it constitutes a valuable backdrop against which I want to recount another story from my family. It is a story by my *father* and of how, whilst he was in a steady relationship with my mother, he was awarded a Queen's Scholarship to pursue further studies overseas. More specifically, it was to pursue a doctorate which would have physically separated him from my mother for many years. And this was at a time when technology did not furnish the tools of rapid communication that we have today.

The Queen's Scholarship was, of course, the highest academic accolade that could be bestowed at that time. It is the equivalent of the President's Scholarship. Like my mother, my father excelled academically. Much more than that, he was an all-rounder who, amongst many other achievements, also represented the then University of Singapore and Singapore itself in field hockey. He was also the School Captain (the highest position of student leadership) in Victoria Institution (the top academic institution in Kuala Lumpur in West Malaysia, where he was born and raised before he came to Singapore for further studies). He obtained a First Class Honours degree in Chemistry from the University of Singapore and was the gold medal recipient in his cohort. Little wonder, then, that the Queen's Scholarship was offered to him.

However, my father turned down this opportunity of a lifetime because he could not bear to be separated from my mother. They were married shortly thereafter. My father had made what one might accurately term a "royal" sacrifice, but it was a sacrifice that he had made unhesitatingly out of his deep love for my mother. Indeed, even when he was working in West Malaysia during the Malayan Emergency (which involved the fight against the Communists), he would drive at breakneck speed in order to avoid the curfews and be together with my mother in Singapore. The end result of all this is a *priceless* love that stretched over six decades. My parents were inseparable and their dedication to each other and to their family have in fact formed the basis for my own approach towards my wife and family. I can, however, honestly say that I have never managed to come close to matching the dedication that my father as well as mother have demonstrated in their love "in action" over so many decades.

Indeed, without my father's unending love for my mother, I would not be here today writing this reflection. Every action has consequences – even far beyond what we can ever imagine with our finite minds. What is clear is that we need to return to *true* romantic love, which is wide as it is deep, and which will (in the nature of things) impact the future to a degree that is even exponential in nature.

True romantic love is bathed in sacrifice.

4

Climbing Ships, Carrying Boys
Parental Love

I have been immensely fortunate. I had parents who loved – and continued, even when I was well into my 60s, to love – me. And although it is true that love is often expressed through words,

words alone are not enough if they are not backed up with actions. In my view, true parental love is embodied in actions and my own fondest memories consist of actions that were not really accompanied by express words. Indeed, one may say that such actions "speak" for themselves – and are louder than mere words could ever be. This may be a particularly important point in an Asian context – especially where fathers of generations past were men of few words. Yet, time and again, we hear children affirming that they felt their fathers' love for them – primarily in working hard and ensuring that they were provided for. I was a little more fortunate. Although what I will describe in this reflection did not involve (for the most part at least) express words, my parents also loved me through their words – not so much in direct words of love but, rather, words of inquiry, words of wisdom as well as words of encouragement. They were, as far as I can remember, always there for me and my siblings, despite their very busy schedules as professionals. We always knew that, when we had a problem, we could always discuss it with them. We were exceedingly fortunate indeed.

As far as specific memories are concerned, there are countless, but I will refer to just a couple – one for each of my parents. My father was a man of considerable talent. I have recounted his scholarly achievements in another reflection.[1] He was professionally capable, but he was also ahead of his time. Whilst respectful of authority, he did not brook nonsense – even though such nonsense could, on occasion, emanate from superiors. He could – and did – stand his ground. He was tough but fair. And above all, his love for his family was unmatched. Although he worked regular hours, he would sometimes return home late from work. The only clue I had was when, on one occasion, I received a comic book from him. He knew I liked reading comics

---

1   See Reflection 3: A 'Royal' Sacrifice, A Priceless Love – True Romantic Love.

and that they were not only very expensive but also not that easy to purchase. That set me wondering where he had obtained the comic from, since his workplace (at the government chemistry department) was as far removed from such publications as one could have imagined.

You see, my father was not only professionally accomplished, he also worked extremely hard to provide for us. And in this last-mentioned regard, unbeknownst to his children, he had, for many years, also climbed up ships to conduct ship inspections. This was no mean feat. It was also unnecessary since my father already earned a more than adequate salary. Decades later, we would learn that his lungs had been somewhat affected as a result of ensuring that the holds of these vessels were free from dangerous gases. My father – like my mother – were persons who, despite their considerable ability, were content not to pursue material wealth or power. They were, however, professionals in every sense of the word. They worked hard for two reasons: they had pride in their work and they wanted to provide for their children as best they could. And that is the standard I have always aspired to emulate. I can honestly say that I have not been as successful but much of my own work ethic can be traced to simple yet profound acts, such as that described here of my father.

As mentioned, my mother is also a lady of considerable talent. She did not only have her knowledge (in chemistry, like my father) at her fingertips but would also (and perhaps as, if not more, importantly) be able to convey it to her students in the clearest of fashions. She had the knack of being simple without being simplistic. Her talent was legendary and she was once even enlisted by a luminary to provide chemistry tuition to his son (who is also now very famous), although she did not believe in giving tuition generally. She only made the rare exception on special occasions and for good reason. Many of her students later became famous in their own right as ministers, doctors, teachers and judges, amongst others. Many would remember her even decades after they had left school. But she was no pushover: like my father, she would stand her ground against unreasonable conduct, even by superiors. I admire both my parents for this quality – the ability to disagree without being intimidated and without being disagreeable. After all, if one cannot live a *principled* life, what is one's life worth?

My own memories, however, are far simpler. Perhaps this is understandable from the perspective of a young child. As I have mentioned in another reflection,[2] her ability to communicate excellently provided me with many life lessons which I now share. But her love – like my father's – was multifaceted. There was an occasion in kindergarten when one of my ankles was caught awkwardly at the bottom of a face-to-face swing. I do not recall it being a massive injury. All I knew was that as I got out of the swing, I suddenly sat down on the grass. I could not move. There was a searing pain and it appeared to be coming from the inside of my ankle. I had suffered a hairline fracture of my ankle through a freak accident. My ankle had to go into a cast. It was most mortifying, especially for a young boy. I could not move around easily. Yet, my mother still endeavoured – despite her busy schedule – to bring me out regularly. To this end, she had to carry me on occasion. It could not have been easy but she never complained. She simply displayed her love for me through her simple actions – actions which had a profound effect on my life. Even as a young child, the impact of her sacrificial love – as with my father's – was conveyed through simple actions rather than large and empty words.

I truly feel blessed to have been showered with so much love by both my parents. If I were to elaborate on this, it would fill up

---

2   See Reflection 1: No Crushed Sugar Cane – How to Treat Others.

at least a small book. They have indeed made me who I am today (the good parts, that is!). Although I later came to realise the role of God as well, I believe that God also provided His love through my parents. They are the standard against which I measure my parenting. I still have some way to go in this regard.

True parental love displays itself in sacrifice.

5
You are Indispensable to Your Family
Importance of Family

What are we defined by? I have found it increasingly the case that many people are defined by their work. I do think that work is important. I believe that we are made – in part – to work in order to not only provide for our families but also live meaningful lives that impact the lives of others in our own special way. However, *extreme views* are – as a general rule of thumb – harmful. And one extreme view is that we are wholly (or even mainly) defined by our work.

Whilst I think that our work does constitute part of who we are, it is (in the final analysis) only a part, and no more. We have often said, "Nobody is indispensable." The irony is that I have noticed that this is a mere empty mantra, which many who utter do not really believe. Although it is perhaps not socially or politically correct to expressly say so, my own suspicion is that, in many cases, people would at least *like to think* that they are indispensable at their workplace. Part of this is due to a point I have just made – that such persons are defined by their work and that, outside their work, they have no real sense of identity or worth. I should hasten to point out at this juncture that we are all afflicted by this misconception at some time or other in our lives. After all, we spend so many of our waking hours at our workplace. The sad fact of the matter, however, is that it is true that "nobody is indispensable". And this applies to *everyone*, *regardless* of the work position we hold. It could be considered to be of a high status (by, of course, the standards of the world), or it could be considered to be the exact opposite (again, by the standards of the world). However, the inescapable fact of the matter is that, should anything happen to us, our employers would always be able to find someone else to replace us and continue the work that we have hitherto been doing. Indeed, the higher the material worth or status of a position, the more persons there would be who are ready and willing to take our place. But this does not mean that we do not do our best at our work. However, what it does mean is that *a sound perspective* is imperative.

And that sound perspective is this: that whilst we are not indispensable at our workplace (and the sooner we internalise this, the (ironically) happier we will be), there is a sense in which we *are* indeed indispensable – *we are indispensable to our families*. To our family members, we are not mere digits who can be easily replaced should something drastic happen to us. We are unique beings, uniquely bonded to each other. We are not easily replaceable – if at all.

And, in this, there is yet another lesson that is, in a sense, closely related. Put simply, it is also true that whilst families constitute the foundation in our network of relationships, broken family relationships can have the opposite effect. That is why it is important, in my view, to try our best to mend family relationships which have somehow gone awry. This is not easy by any means. However, family relationships are so precious that it is worth making the effort to do so. When all is said and done, it is these relationships that go beyond the mundane and which – in a very real sense – help make us who we are.

> *Whilst we are not indispensable at*
> *the workplace, we are indispensable*
> *to our respective families.*

6

Walking Around in
Someone Else's Skin
Perspectives

I first read the famous novel, *To Kill A Mockingbird*, when I was in Secondary 3. It was prescribed reading for our literature course. And, to this day, I am so glad that it was. It is so famous because it contains so much texture on the nature of human relationships – both good and bad. After I had read law, I realised that there was even more in this particular book than I had once thought. Its richness constitutes an excellent base from which to explore human relationships and human nature. There are therefore many invaluable lessons contained in this text. In particular, there is one that I found so relevant that it has stayed with me ever since I first read it. I have even used it in a Law School Commencement Speech that I delivered some years back.

The lesson I am referring to is contained in a specific quotation which consists of advice from a father to his daughter, and which is as follows:[3]

> First of all, ... if you can learn a simple trick,
> Scout, you'll get along a lot better with all kinds
> of folks. You never really understand a person

---

3   *To Kill A Mockingbird* (J B Lippincott Company, 1960) at p 33.

until you consider things from his point of view
– … until you climb into his skin and walk
around in it.

But what does it mean? I think it means that, before we are
too quick to pass judgment on someone else, we should look at
things from that particular person's perspective or point of view.
This particular quotation makes the point even more starkly,
in my view, because it talks about actually "climbing into" that
particular person's "skin" in order to "walk around in it". You
see, the trouble with the human psyche is that we are selfish by
nature. More than that, our egos are – whether we like to admit it
or not – rather large. There is therefore a very natural tendency to
insist that our views are the only correct views. I believe that most
misunderstandings arise as a result of our own blinkered approach
and our refusal to at least try to look at a contrary view through the
other person's lenses. Indeed, walking around in someone's skin is
not the same thing as getting under that person's skin. Most of the
time, however, it is the latter that results – because we are so cock-
sure of our views, we attempt to impose it on the other party, thus
getting under that person's skin instead!

I believe that it is not only in situations of potential (or even
actual) conflict that such an approach is useful. Even when one is
at the planning stage of a project, it is useful to ask oneself how
a particular approach that might be adopted would be received
by others who are affected by it. This would also serve to reassure
oneself that one is being fair and objective in proffering a certain
line of approach to a specific project or matter.

This is such a simple and even obvious point that readers
may wonder why I am even bothering to raise it in the first
place. However, from my own personal experience, this point is
not as obvious as one would think – if the many (unnecessary)
disagreements that occur between persons (whether at home or at

the workplace or even with strangers) are anything to go by. It is also not something that would come easily to everyone. For those who are naturally empathetic, this would not pose a problem at all and would probably be part and parcel of their dealings with others. For some individuals, however, it is something that ought to be learnt as well as practised because, once it becomes a natural part of the way in which we interact with others, it can prove to be a real boon to all concerned.

Before judging others, always step into their shoes and view things from their perspective first.

7

Little Kindnesses
Power of Kindness

Unlike many persons, I thought that I would remain in my job at a particular university for life. After all, one main part of it (relating to research) was something that was such a natural fit and the other (relating to teaching), whilst less of a strength, was nevertheless something I believed in and therefore had a commitment to. This did not mean that there were no difficulties. Indeed, there were many but that is life (and the topic for another reflection). As the days passed into months and into years, and then into decades, what I had thought at first appeared to be a reality. However, little did I know that almost two decades into the first job I ever had, I was due to change jobs. It was not overly traumatic in the sense that I would be switching into a similar (academic) job but any change after almost two decades of clear routine would necessarily be somewhat disconcerting and even disruptive. It was not an easy decision to make but once the die was cast, there was no turning back.

I recall sending an e-mail to all the staff, many of whom I had known for close to two decades. It was not an easy one to send. As I looked back at my time at that university, my mind turned very naturally to the two main themes that constituted the foundation of my job: research and teaching. There was a pretty substantial record of the former and, whilst I cannot pretend to have been the best teacher (because I did not believe in "spoon-feeding" and I always tried to stretch my students that little bit further), there was sufficient satisfaction in my commitment to not just teaching my students the requisite material but also about life itself. I did not expect much of a response, though, to my e-mail. I was to be surprised – in more ways than one.

In the first place, I received far more responses than I had expected. More importantly, though, the *content* of those responses gave me a wholly different perspective on one particular aspect of life. You see, I had expected my former colleagues to lament the loss of my research contributions and perhaps even my (allegedly misplaced) concern for my students in their respective life journeys. But what I received was *completely different*. Without going into particular details, what underlay many of the responses centred on *little kindnesses that (for the colleague concerned) defined his or her view of me and my role in their respective lives*. This stunned me because, like many, I used to believe that we are defined by the so-called "big things" in life. Many of the little kindnesses mentioned were precisely that – "little". I must confess that it took me more than a little while to recall a few of the situations concerned – so trivial they had seemed to me at the time. However, with the benefit of hindsight, I realised that, what appeared little or trivial to myself at the time meant something significant to the person concerned. I then realised that, on many such occasions, I had (subconsciously at least) realised that there was a need for just a kind word or two, or just being present to listen. I also realised that perhaps we are not, in the final analysis, defined by the so-called "big things" we do in life. Indeed, for the most part, I have now come to see that we do these things for ourselves and to make ourselves – not others – feel good or worthwhile.

At the end of our lives, however, I now believe that we will not be remembered for these "big things" but, rather (if at all), for the so-called "little things" we do for others, the little kindnesses that we show along life's path (which, at the material time, may turn out to matter a lot to the person concerned). And, if we can internalise this as an *attitude of life* (if nothing else, so as not to become self-conscious and self-conceited), we would have achieved what we have each been placed on this earth to do – to somehow make a difference in the lives of others with whom we have been placed in touch. It might not seem like much simply because it cannot be quantified. However, I have learnt that the most significant things in life cannot be quantified. It is true that it requires a certain amount of faith to persevere since there is no empirical test as such. However, ever so often, there *is* some confirmation (or even affirmation), although (for me at least) it took me close to two decades for this to happen.

Never underestimate the power
of little kindnesses.

8

Before it is Too Late
Not Procrastinating

Many of us are procrastinators by nature. I am an exception – although my family thinks that, by constantly pressing on, I am placing too much stress on myself as well as those around me. It is true that part of my problem is fear: in particular, the fear that, if things are left too late, they will somehow go horribly wrong. I confess that this is not a good reason for constantly being on one's bicycle, so to speak. Indeed, in another reflection, I talk about the importance of sleep.[4] However, it is equally true that procrastination is an undesirable trait. To simply let a task drag along does not mean that that task will somehow go away. Often, it only gets larger and larger – until it might become even unmanageable. However, procrastination is even more undesirable when it comes to *relationships*. I learnt this the hard way.

When I was a young lecturer, I was tasked to teach jurisprudence or legal philosophy. I must say that it was my favourite subject as a student. I liked analysing legal doctrine but its underlying conceptual framework or theory fascinated me even more. I should state that it was – by its very nature – an extremely difficult subject to teach. Because it was so abstract and involved, I thought that – much as I liked teaching the subject – I was unlikely to ever write

---

4   See Reflection 30: Rest for Life – Sleep.

on it. After all, the books and articles I had read out of interest as well as in preparation for my classes were all so difficult to understand. What I did do, however, was to read all the classic jurisprudence texts in much greater detail than I had when I was a student. This was only to be expected since I needed to know the entire terrain well in order to guide my students through it. One of these books was a classic then (as it is now) in legal philosophy. It was entitled *The Concept of Law*, and had been authored by an extremely famous Oxford Professor, Professor H L A Hart.

As I re-read Professor Hart's book, I came across a chapter that I had never read before and which was seldom prescribed for students. Yet, it was in the pages of that very chapter that I found passages which led me to think that the very famous jurisprudential debate between Professor Hart and his successor to the Chair of Jurisprudence at Oxford, the American legal philosopher, Professor Ronald Dworkin, was – at its root – a misconceived one since it seemed to me that Professor Dworkin had quite clearly attributed to Professor Hart a view that he did not hold (or at least did not hold in such stark terms as merited criticism by Professor Dworkin). This was one of the points that came to my mind as I re-read the book. There was another point that related to yet another very famous jurisprudential debate that was even older than the one I have just mentioned, between Professor Hart and Professor Lon L Fuller of Harvard Law School. I thought that this particular debate was not really a debate at all because both Professor Hart and Professor Fuller were – in substance – speaking at cross-purposes; put simply, there was no real debate that they could join issue on.

In the enthusiasm (or, perhaps more accurately, recklessness) of youth, I wrote a letter to Professor Hart with regard to both these debates. I think that, deep down inside, I thought that I had nothing to lose. However, also deep down inside, I was firmly of the view that I would never receive a reply. After all, why would a world-renowned professor reply to a young lecturer teaching literally thousands of miles away?

Some weeks passed and I received a letter. I still remember it to this day. It was in a light blue envelope. More strikingly, my name and address were written in impeccable penmanship – it was also obvious that it had been written in fountain pen. I opened the letter. The first thing that caught my eye were the words right at the top of the letter: "From the desk of H L A Hart". Within it, in densely packed handwritten words that covered both sides of a sheet of note paper was succinct – yet highly perceptive – analysis of the two issues I had raised in my letter to him. I was utterly stunned for a moment. As mentioned, I had sent the letter without ever expecting a response. And here I was – letter in hand – with detailed responses to my queries. I was humbled – not least by the humility of a scholar who took the trouble to write back to an utterly unknown lecturer situated thousands of miles distant. This reply furnished me with the confidence to write and publish my very first article in jurisprudence.

But this is not the nub of the present reflection. A year or two later, I was on sabbatical leave and was visiting the law school at Bristol to meet with Professor Michael Furmston who was (at the time of writing, although, sadly, he has since passed away) the editor of the world famous contract text, *Cheshire, Fifoot and Furmston's Law of Contract*. I was working on a Singapore and Malaysian edition of this book. I had heard from a senior professor at Oxford that Professor Hart was in declining health. I had thought of travelling there to personally thank him for his kindness in responding to my letter. But I felt embarrassed. How would he receive me? Would he think me too bold? But these were, as I later realised, mere excuses used to (feebly) justify my procrastination. I never did make that one-hour journey across from Bristol to Oxford. Not long after my return, I heard that he had passed away. I was stunned this time around as well, but for a wholly different reason. It was a significant lesson for me. When I subsequently published an article on the Postscript in the second edition of *The Concept of Law* (which was itself published posthumously), I added an acknowledgment of Professor Hart's kindness and graciousness. But it was not the same thing as personally thanking him. I learnt a really important lesson from this particular experience and I never procrastinated again – especially when thanking persons who had taken the trouble to extend kindness to me.

I related this story, on occasion, to my jurisprudence students. On one occasion, I found that it had applications beyond the expression of gratitude for kindnesses received. I do not know what prompted it, but I suddenly added this – that, for many of us, there are more negative experiences that have befallen us. Many (unfortunately) concern (broken) relationships with even loved ones. It seemed to me that the warning against procrastination applied to such relationships as well, perhaps with even greater force. To effect closure and even make peace in such situations is tough to do, but is, I strongly believe, a valuable experience. Above all, achieving closure on a personal level leaves no room for later regrets. I would highly recommend it.

It is unwise to procrastinate either in expressing gratitude for kindness received or in effecting closure in the context of broken relationships. Never leave things too late, lest there be a lifetime of regrets.

9

Receiving the Wisdom of the Ages
Importance of Mentorship

I must confess that I had not – for the longest time – realised the importance of wise mentorship. If I may be brutally frank and honest, the concept of mentoring others is not high on the list of many people. This is perhaps understandable in light of the harsh world in which we live where many are concerned only (or, in fairness, mainly) with their own selfish ambitions and ends. That is why we often speak of the "rat race" – a condition perhaps exacerbated nowadays when there is so much more unnecessary stress (often ironically justified in the name of "progress").

If I am truly honest, I cannot say that I have had much – at least systematic – mentorship in my life. That having been said, I was extremely fortunate. Unbeknownst to myself, I was actually receiving wise mentorship from my parents. As I have mentioned on more than one occasion, I would not be the person I am today without their wise advice and guidance throughout my life (even as an adult).[5] And this was all to the good because I can say that in my more than four decades of working life, I have often had to learn from my own experience (on occasion at least, quite bitter experience). It would have been so much better to have had someone mentor me on a systematic basis. This having been said,

---

5   See also Reflection 4: Climbing Ships, Carrying Boys – Parental Love.

my wife has always been a source of love and wise advice. I have also had colleagues who have provided me with wise advice from time to time. On the spiritual plane, I have also had the wisdom and counsel of a dear and close friend (who perhaps, next to my parents and my wife, I count as someone whom I would truly consider to have been a mentor).

As already mentioned, the world can be a very tough place to negotiate – on occasion, it can even be a kind of wild jungle, fraught with pitfalls and dangers. That perhaps sums up the imperfect world that we live in. It can – especially when we are young – be particularly daunting when we are faced with specific difficulties or problems, but have no appropriate person to whom we can turn for advice. I have myself had numerous difficult experiences – particularly during my younger days – when I was, quite frankly, "drowning". If not for family and God, I might well indeed have gone under and would not be here today writing the present reflection. Indeed, some instances are described in other reflections in this book.

However, the difficult situations just alluded to had, in my view, a more than silver lining. When one faces difficulties and, in particular, injustice, one should, as I have reflected elsewhere,[6] forget about the injustice lest it festers and destroys oneself and also endeavour to not only forget but also forgive as well. I would suggest a yet further lesson from my own experience in encountering injustice and unfairness. It taught me not only how *not* to conduct myself but also how (and on a more *positive* note) I *ought to* conduct myself. To this last-mentioned end, I have always (albeit not always successfully) endeavoured to advise others in need to the best of my ability. And this is, I believe, the *attitude* that we must cultivate if we are to equip ourselves as possible mentors. Mentoring is, of course, far more extensive and, in a

---

6   See Reflection 20: Beneficial 'Forgetfulness' – Handling Injustice.

word, *systematic* – stemming from a *relationship* that is established between mentor and mentee alike.

The ideal for each and every one of us is – if it is at all possible – to be mentored by someone wiser and, in turn, to pay that forward, so to speak, by mentoring others in turn. This does not mean that we should be anxiously seeking either to be mentored or to mentor, but when the correct person and moment arrives, we should be prepared to assume either role as is appropriate. I should also add that being a mentor does not require exceptional abilities, although it does require empathy and a desire to help others. Often, just a listening ear and a kind heart as well as words of wise advice would suffice. Modelling by example is also yet another way of mentoring, as deeds often speak even louder than words. I truly believe that all this is within the capacity of each and every one of us.

> *We should, if the appropriate opportunities arise, both be mentored wisely and mentor wisely in turn.*

VALUES AND DISCIPLINES

10

Always Do the Right Thing
Integrity

This was amongst the final reflections I had written for this book. It ought really to have been the first. The reason why I had not thought to include a reflection on integrity was probably because I had assumed that this was so obvious that it did not need to be included. I was wrong. A number of fairly recent events (including cheating at professional law examinations) has demonstrated that integrity is not always a value which is consciously practised. This is rather unfortunate. I believe that one possible reason that this is the case is the all too human tendency towards selfishness (often embodied in the phrase "looking after number one"). Another closely related reason is the increasingly popular view that everything is subjective and that one is therefore free to do whatever one pleases since there is no objective morality.

I fully understand the first reason. We all tend to be selfish and desire what is best for ourselves. As already mentioned, this is an all too human trait. However, might I suggest that there is a countervailing human trait that is quite different in orientation – that it is laudable to give to others, especially those in need. Whilst we need not go so far as to engage in unbridled altruism, the value of *integrity* dictates that there are *limits* to the lengths to which we can go in order to feather our own nests. Whatever we do must be grounded on a principled basis – in particular, that of honesty. Put simply, we must always do the right thing, even if it is contrary to our own self-interests. And it is best to practise such a quality *holistically*. Nothing is too small in this regard.

I recall once realising that excess change had been given to me at a store. The difference was a small one. I had already walked some distance from the store and it seemed tempting to rationalise away the need to make the trip back and to queue all over again – merely to return some change. I continued walking but something gnawed within me. I turned and trudged back to the store. As expected, there was a queue. I joined it, only for the cashier to look at me in astonishment when it was my turn because I had no item for purchase. I then explained to him that I was coming back to return some excess change. He looked stunned for a moment and then muttered, "Honest guy!" I relate this story not to praise myself. On the contrary, in my view, there is nothing praiseworthy in doing the right thing. The amount involved in this episode may have been small but it was the *principle* that mattered most. Indeed, if we are not prepared to be honest and to do right in small things, there is a great likelihood that we might not do right in bigger things. I should add that *true* integrity lies in the decision to do the right thing *even when nobody is looking and there is the no risk of being discovered if one decides to act otherwise.*

Another example relates to telling the truth. I have noticed the people who lie and who refuse to own up to the truth tend to lie in order to cover up their actions. In most instances, the person concerned is caught in an even larger web of lies, which is most unfortunate, to say the least.

This brings me to the second possible reason why some people may not practise integrity – the perception that everything is subjective. I can deal with this very shortly and on a very logical level. There is in truth no such thing as complete subjectivity simply because the proposition that everything is subjective is itself an *objective* statement as well as claim. Unfortunately, it is a most impoverished one indeed![7] In my view, it is far better to subscribe to the proposition (or, rather, principle) of always being honest and doing the right thing – even if it might be contrary to one's self-interest.

> *One should always be honest and do the*
> *right thing – even if doing so might be*
> *contrary to one's self-interest.*

11

Do Your Best, Regardless …

True Excellence

There appears nowadays to be so much emphasis on excellence that the *true* meaning of that term appears to have taken on many shades of meaning. For some, it is attaining high material status; for others, it is earning as much money as possible; for yet others, it is a combination of both of these definitions. These are, in fact, the "popular" views of what excellence means nowadays.

What I would like to suggest, however, is something completely different. I want to suggest what, in my view, constitutes *true* excellence: conducting ourselves in a manner that gives true meaning and purpose to what we do in our workplace and as human beings – for the one is inextricably connected to the other. More concretely, we must always do our very best, regardless of where we are and the task which has been allotted to us *and* we must trust that what we do will touch lives for the better. This applies not only in the work context but also the family context as well. Trusting that we have touched lives for the better is, in my view, of vital importance because, as I have already mentioned at the outset of this reflection, we often measure one's significance by the professional heights we have reached in terms of status, power and material wealth. Let me suggest that this is an erroneous approach, not least because it means that the vast majority of us could never find meaning, significance or purpose in our lives. Such an approach also ignores the fact that true success in touching lives cannot be measured by such a simplistic metric and, indeed, cannot often be measured at all. Let me elaborate from my own experience.

When I was a mere clerk in the army, I nevertheless strove to do the best I could. That is why, to this day, I still recall being so quietly proud at having my perfect copy typescript pinned up on the class noticeboard whilst attending an advanced clerk course. It was nothing in itself but it was symbolic of the fact that by sheer determination and practice, I managed to overcome my inherent lack of manual dexterity and was able to contribute in my small way. Put simply, I was determined to be the best clerk that I could be.

When I entered law school, I was determined to be the best law student I could be. Believe it or not, grades were not the primary motivation because there were many courses in which an A grade was not awarded.

When I began lecturing in law school, my mother, who was a gifted teacher and principal, was appalled that I would be "unleashed" on my unsuspecting students after only two days of lectures at the then Institute of Education. Notwithstanding that, I tried – for well over two decades – to be the best lecturer I could be, caring for my students not merely as receptacles to be filled with legal knowledge but also as people to engage with not just on law but also on life itself. The law is a marvellous vehicle for discussing life and life values (without, of course, imposing one's own views in a dogmatic fashion). I also strove to be the best researcher I could be. Put simply, I embraced legal academia as a real calling.

It came as a bolt from the blue when I was asked to join the Bench. I then strove to be the best judge that I could be. It was not an easy task at first. Indeed, after joining the Bench, I recall being in Hong Kong to deliver a public lecture. One of the first questions I was asked was what it was like to be a judge after having been a legal academic for such a long time. I still recall my response vividly. It was unscripted and instinctive but quite picturesque. I likened the initial transition as follows: being a legal academic was like wearing gloves that were crafted by its maker who knew not only the size of my hands but also the best material from which to craft those gloves, with the material fitting so well that it felt like it was a part of me, whereas being a judge was like climbing up an almost perpendicular wall with no safety harness! I am grateful that after so many years now on the Bench, the experience generates much less apprehension.

What I draw from my life's journey is, first, that life is unpredictable. As alluded to earlier, not all of us will reach the pinnacle of material success. In my view, however, that does not prevent us from having lives filled with meaning and purpose. Had I continued as a clerk or a secretary (as in the army), I would still have tried to be the best clerk or secretary I could be and would have found meaning in being just that. And, as already mentioned, I strove to be the best lecturer I could be and had I remained in legal academia, I would have been content in finding meaning in that calling. Indeed, as I reflected upon each stage of my life's journey, the *attitude* has been the same. As importantly, I have always made it a point to make time for my family. Nobody is indispensable at the workplace but we are indispensable to our families.

But, you may ask, how then do we measure whether we have touched other lives? It might be easier to discern this in our family context for obvious reasons. That is why I mentioned that we must *trust* that our efforts have touched other lives (including those of clients). I believe that as I was given, you, too, will be given tangible encouragement along the way – and that will keep you going. For example, I believe that I was not the most popular lecturer because I did not believe in spoon-feeding my students but, on occasion, I would receive a heartfelt card or letter and that kept me going. I have taken some time to emphasise that we must always do our very best, regardless of where we are and the task which has been allotted to us *and* we must trust that what we do will touch lives for the better – and that this applies not only in the professional context but also the family context as well – because I believe that this life principle will help sustain you, dear reader, in your professional and life journeys. It has certainly sustained me for over four decades. In my view, this is not mere blue sky idealism but you need to have the courage to *live* it out in order to validate it through your own tangible experience.

Books, articles and judgments will become outdated with time. You can leave behind material wealth but you cannot take it with you. However, the life you have touched (even if the person concerned does not thank you expressly) is part of a *living legacy*. Whilst you might not be able to measure success in this context in conventional terms, I believe that if you have touched even one life for the better, that is more precious than all the material accolades in the world (and it will be very likely that you have in fact touched far more lives than that). This is not to downplay those who are indeed materially successful but if you happen to fall into this category, wear your honours lightly and use your talents and resources to enrich the lives of others. Above all, never neglect your family – value them and love them – for they are irreplaceable to you as you are to them.

True excellence is always doing one's best
– regardless of where we are – in order to
touch the lives of others for the better.

12

Being Transparent

Sincerity

As with the reflection on integrity,[8] I never thought initially to include a reflection on sincerity (or, in alternative and more contemporary parlance, authenticity). Again, I was of the view that such a quality was so obvious that it did not need to be the subject of a reflection. On further consideration, however, it became more and more obvious that although I had always taken such a quality for granted, it was not as widely practised as it ought to be. Indeed, I was reminded of a couple of situations from my own experience.

The first was the fact that somehow I generally got on well with older folk (although I now belong to that category as well!). I took this for granted until one day, I realised that one possible reason for this was because I was always sincere and open and that older people especially appreciated this (having had more experience in discerning the sincere from the insincere). I, too, can now understand why, having lived for several more decades since. Having been raised by my parents to be always polite and genuine as well as sincere, it seemed second nature to me to be always direct and straightforward (albeit with courtesy when the occasion demanded it). However, having also been in the real world, so to speak, for so many decades, I have discovered that people are not always straightforward.

The second situation was rather more specific. A person who was leaving for another job dropped by to see me and surprised me by stating how much she appreciated me even though I did not have very many dealings with her. In particular, she mentioned that I would always remember her name. This shocked me greatly – after all, was it not polite to remember someone's name, regardless of his or her rank in the organisation concerned? She went on to state that this made her feel valued as an individual and not merely as a cog in the institutional machine.

In point of fact, people are generally not stupid. Far from it. And educational level or material status is irrelevant. Indeed, some of the wisest people I know did not attain a high educational level and/or high material status. Put simply, people know sincerity or authenticity when they see it. By the same token, even though they may not (understandably) articulate it, they also know insincerity when they encounter it. I am not, however, stating that one should feign or pretend to be sincere. Far from it. In the first place and as just mentioned, most people will see through such conduct. More importantly perhaps, sincerity or authenticity might sometimes entail being direct and telling another person what he or she might *not* like to hear. In such situations, however (and as alluded to briefly above), one should convey such information with sensitivity and empathy. At the end of the day, all that is required of us is the ability to be transparent with others. As I often tell others, with me, what they see is what they get – no more, and no less.

One should always be transparent and
sincere, regardless of the situation.

13

Yesterday's Newspaper Headlines, Today's Fish and Chips Wrappers
Fame and Humility

I refer to another of my mother's stories which is also deeply etched in my memory. However, before I do so, I must observe that it always seemed to me that humility was not merely a desirable trait – I thought that it was necessary. Over the years, I have discovered (unfortunately) that humility is not that common a quality as I had thought. Perhaps it is due to modern society – in particular, that one cannot show weakness but, instead, must impress by catching everyone's attention. On further reflection, I realised that the need to be humble was something that might not have come naturally to me had I been left to my own devices – it was ingrained in me by my parents. I think that much also depends on one's inherent character. I am a shy person by nature. I have learnt to come out of my shell, so to speak, over the years but my inherent shyness leads me more along the road of humility rather than arrogance. The only danger in this regard (if I may be permitted to digress) is to fall into the equally undesirable trap of false modesty. It therefore becomes essential to always maintain a balance in life.

Returning to the present story, my mother mentioned to us more than once that fame is – at best – temporary and ephemeral. To illustrate this, she referred to fish and chips or,

more accurately, to the newspapers which were used to wrap
fish and chips. Some context might be in order here. When I
was very young, my father and mother – with myself as a baby
in tow – went to England as my father was pursuing a Masters
degree in Chemistry. As many readers would know, fish and
chips is a very famous meal in England. And, traditionally,
servings of fish and chips are (or at least were then) wrapped in
newspapers. Somehow, the newsprint was of a superior quality
that enabled them to absorb any excess oil from the meal. I do
not think that the same would obtain in Singapore – especially
with the added disadvantage of the natural heat and humidity.
But, again, I digress. My mother's point was an exceedingly
simple and straightforward one – fame, like newspaper headlines,
might provide one with a heady feeling for a time, but it is only

temporary. The next day's newspaper headlines emerge and those of yesterday are often forgotten immediately. Indeed, the entire newspaper of the previous day becomes redundant. Well, as my mother put it, perhaps not entirely so – because it can then be used to wrap fish and chips!

I must say that this particular illustration – a kind of "word picture", if you will – struck me immediately. Indeed, we are all impressed by newspaper headlines. Headlines, by their very nature, draw attention to the individuals featured therein – whether for better or worse. When, of course, it is the former, it "bathes" the individual concerned in fame. But it is true that such fame is, in the final analysis, only temporary at best. I can testify to this from both observation as well as personal experience. When one is successful in a material sense, many people want to know you; and the converse is more often than not the case when one is unsuccessful. Indeed, one need not even have to be perceived as being unsuccessful – just being average would suffice to "blend" one, as it were, into the background and obscurity.

This is yet another reason why I think it is *necessary* to be humble. In point of fact, any fame we garner is only temporary – even more temporary than the clothes we wear. So we must "wear" any fame we have with humility. And there is no better way to ensure that this is the case than to try to use whatever fame is conferred upon us to help others – in a sense, to reflect that fame away from us so that someone else (especially someone in need) receives attention instead. I can state unhesitatingly that this is not an easy thing to do. In my view, it has to do with human nature. Humans are essentially rather selfish and we tend, therefore, to look after ourselves and our loved ones rather than others. Why we should help others is something I will deal in another reflection.[9] For present purposes, it will suffice to emphasise once again that

---

9   See Reflection 29: Mountain Top or Mountain Help? – Further Reflection on Meaning of Success.

we all need to handle fame with a light touch and focus on being humble instead.

Not surprisingly, when I became a Christian, I found that the desirable values as well as attitude I have just mentioned were not considered to be something exceptional – it was an expected part of the Christian life. Throughout the Bible, we are told to be humble and that God opposes the proud but exalts the humble. I found, though, that what has just been stated may not come to pass in a literal – or, more accurately, worldly or material – way. The Christian's reward is not necessarily or always a material one but what he or she can be assured of is that there are rewards that transcend even the highest worldly accolades when one passes on into eternity. I was gratified, though, to learn that all that I had been taught by my parents and that I had attempted my level best to practise was not only consistent with my newly found faith but that I could also look to God and the Holy Spirit for the wisdom, guidance as well as strength to practise these values.

Worldly fame, like fish and chips wrappers, is only temporary. Humility, however, is necessary and enduring.

14

Uncommon Wisdom
Meaning of Wisdom

"Wisdom" has often been conflated with "knowledge". Whilst knowledge is indeed important (not least to help us function in the world in which we live), it is, however, *not* the same as wisdom. Nevertheless, I have come across many instances where wisdom has been associated with extreme cleverness that has at its base a storehouse of secular knowledge. However, wisdom is not mere cleverness because at its root, human nature is filled with ego and its consequent arrogance. There are, as a result, many extremely clever people who have much knowledge but who, because of their overinflated opinion of themselves, lack true wisdom. What, then, is wisdom?

Wisdom is the quality of having good judgment that allows one to apply the relevant knowledge in the most appropriate and effective manner possible. However, in my view at least, there is a fundamental requirement that must be satisfied before one can even be considered to have good judgment in this stated manner. It is *humility*. As alluded to above, the bane of human nature consists in its natural tendency towards ego, towards being puffed up and being caught up in the conceit of one's knowledge and, possibly, status as well. The great difficulty is that this is a very insidious process. The vast majority of us do not even realise that we are being puffed up. However, like a disease, the tendency that culminates in arrogance has an inexorable life of its own if it is not checked. And perhaps the most effective way of checking this is by adopting a consistent posture of humility. This is, of course, easier said than done. A good rule of thumb from my own experience, though, lies in the saying (often attributed to Aristotle) that "The more you know, the more you do not know." Indeed, even as I delved more and more into a specialised area of law as a legal academic, I found that the more I learnt as well as reflected, the more issues and questions I had and that I was, as a result, very wary of being called an expert in the field. And if that applies to one narrow and specialised area, what more other areas of knowledge and of life itself?

It is, however, not easy to maintain a constant posture of humility. Fortunately, and speaking for myself, I draw my strength from Someone higher than myself (as I have mentioned in another related reflection).[10] Again, speaking for myself, I could never be *truly* humble were I to rely upon myself because it is "myself" that constitutes the source of the problem in the first place. On a closely related note, I was very struck by the fact that my elder daughter had, when she was very young, asked my wife what the difference was between cleverness and wisdom. After my wife had explained the difference, she asked my wife to pray not only that she be clever but also (and more importantly) that she be wise. And this was no mere mantra she learnt from the church as she understood precisely what she was requesting. Perhaps in order to be truly wise, one must adopt an almost child-like (as opposed to childish) approach. Indeed, the pool of knowledge has exploded (since Aristotle's time) and many people in the world view knowledge as an end in itself rather than as a means to help others. May we

---

10   See also Reflection 13: Yesterday's Newspaper Headlines, Today's Fish and Chips Wrappers – Fame and Humility.

all understand what *true* wisdom is by first adopting a constant posture of humility. May we also always address our minds as to how to *apply* whatever knowledge we have *for the benefit of others* (as opposed to ourselves). Such wisdom is not, as I have alluded to, as common as we would like, hence my reference in the title of this reflection to the term "uncommon wisdom".

> *True wisdom transcends mere knowledge and is, in fact, the humble application of that knowledge for the benefit of others.*

15

A Life that Goes Over into Other Lives

Imparting Wisdom

When I entered law school, I never thought that I would be a "teacher". Ironically (and this was a point that my mother, an excellent teacher in her own right as I have noted earlier in this book,[11] did point out to me right at the commencement of my career in legal academia), I did not – unlike teachers in school – receive much formal training. It was, if my memory serves me correctly, a two-day course – and that was the sum total of my training before I was plunged into the lecture theatre and tutorial room proper. Put simply, I had to learn on the job. In fact, it is here, in the more informal classroom of life itself that we learn how to impart not only our knowledge but also our wisdom to others: in particular, to our children. And in imparting such lessons (in particular, lessons about how to live life meaningfully), I found that there was no better – and frightening – method than to *demonstrate it through one's life*. It took me a little time, but I soon found out that, as a lecturer, I was scrutinised by some students as one would look at a goldfish in a bowl. I discovered this principally when my teaching evaluations came in. Not surprisingly, they were often mixed – which is why I was much

---

11 See Reflection 1: No Crushed Sugar Cane – How to Treat Others.

happier to receive thank-you cards instead. Unfortunately, they were in somewhat short supply.

Returning to formal teaching proper, perhaps I can do no better than to relate my own experience as a law lecturer – a job (I prefer to refer to it as a calling) which occupied almost the first quarter of a century of my working life. And I draw, here, from some personal reflections in an essay which I co-wrote a few years ago.

It seems like just yesterday when I was a fresh graduate eagerly, and even passionately, embarking on an academic career. It sounds like a cliché, but it was all so very true (and rings true to me even today). My only ambition then was to be as good a legal researcher and a law teacher as I could. It was a career in which I felt a real calling. It is an experiential matter which is difficult to capture in mere words, save to say that it not only felt right but also felt as if I had been born to do it (whether or not it benefitted the recipients of my efforts!). This was certainly the case for legal research. I was always interested in the law and loved writing about it (right from my first year as a student in law school). Teaching displayed less objective evidence. I never won a teaching award, but there is one thing I was always sure about – whether they realised it or not, I cared for my students not merely as receptacles to be filled with legal knowledge (although that is, I must concede, a not unimportant function of a law lecturer, second, of course, to making students *think* about the law) but also as people to engage with not just on law but also on life itself. The law is, in fact, a marvellous vehicle for discussing life and life values (without imposing one's own personal views, of course). I cannot say that I was successful in any substantial measure, but at least I tried and I did receive the occasional feedback, often years or decades down the road, either orally or in writing.

It seems strange to cite anything from a film as I am not a film buff and seldom go to the cinema. However, there is one memorable line from a film that was by no means an international hit but which seems to me to encapsulate the essence of the ideal teacher. The film is entitled *The Emperor's Club*, and was based on a short story by Ethan Canin (entitled "The Palace Thief"). Towards the end of the film, one of the students reads the following tribute from a plaque which he presents on behalf of the rest of his cohort to their former teacher:

> A great teacher has little external history to record. His life goes over into other lives. These men[12] are pillars in the intimate structure of our schools. They are more essential than its stones or beams, and they will continue to be a kindling force and a revealing power in our lives.

However, what of the future? For me, there is not that much more time – relatively speaking – for active contributions on my part.[13] The legal baton must be passed, and rightly so. On a personal level, I am most encouraged for the future because it will be manned by persons more capable than I. That is not only consistent with the ideals of a teacher which I have referred to above, but is also consistent with the ideals of succession generally. Vanity and ego are great stumbling blocks in life, whereas humility and sacrifice are utterly necessary for the growth not only of individuals but also of society itself. It will not be an easy road. I used, on occasion, to tell my students that my hope was that they would contribute much in positions of significance and authority in the future, but that my greatest worry was that they might get too caught up with their own selfish ambitions once they attained positions of

---

12 It should be noted that the teacher concerned in this film was male.
13 Indeed, the author has since retired from his appointment as a full-time judge.

authority. To overcome this obstacle is easier said than done: the vanity and ego I have just referred to are often insidious influences (and often self-rationalised). However, the paradox, in my view, is that by discarding selfish ambition, one can achieve true greatness by – to borrow from the above quotation – ensuring that one's life goes into or flows into other lives, impacting them for the better.

> *Imparting wisdom requires us to*
> *live wisely ourselves, pouring*
> *our lives into other lives.*

16

Do Not Hurry; Do Stop and Reflect
Patience

There is no denying the fact that we live in an increased – and increasingly – busy and hurried world. This is especially evident in large cities where people not only live cheek by jowl but also appear to be always in a rush. Not surprisingly, such impatience leads to actions (and consequences) that nobody ought to be proud of. It also takes a heavy toll on oneself as the body and mind, amongst other things, are stressed.

I must confess to having this "disease" of impatience myself. And it manifests itself in at least two ways. The first is outward-looking and is directed towards others. Because of the fast pace of life, there is, on occasion, the tendency to feel impatience at the fact that others have not responded to oneself. Such a tendency could well be subconscious in nature – for example, I sometimes find myself checking and rechecking my e-mail, which is an obvious concern to receive a response that has not arrived yet. The second manifestation is inward-looking and, in my situation at least, is far more harmful – it is the tendency to be impatient with oneself (sometimes itself a manifestation, in turn, of the also harmful tendency towards perfectionism). The tendency towards impatience with *oneself* is even more harmful because one is often not conscious of it. Put simply, it results in one being overly hard on oneself. What, then, is the solution towards impatience in its various forms?

I think that the first step towards a possible solution is one that is common to dealing with many other difficult traits – a *consciousness* that (here) impatience is a very real danger. Once one is conscious of the danger of impatience, the next step, I believe, is having the *discipline* to deal with it. Now, both these steps are unnecessary in the rare instance when a person – by his or her very disposition or natural make up – is patient. However, this is more the exception rather than the rule and, as alluded to above, I certainly do not (unfortunately) fall within this rare category. Hence, I sometimes find it necessary to curb a "natural" tendency towards impatience through exercising self-discipline. After a while, though, I discovered that through the exercise of such self-discipline, it became easier to be patient without engaging in overt and artificial acts of self-discipline. This actually enabled me to work better and also ensured that others who interacted with me were treated fairly and even kindly.

More generally speaking, though, all of us ought, in my view, to hurry less and stop and reflect more. Acting in this more measured way will also do our bodies and minds a world of good. More than that, as already mentioned, I believe that such an approach towards life will actually enable us to be more efficient as well as productive, and, more importantly, treat others in a more humane fashion. This is not an easy task, though, and will, as I have alluded to above, require the exercise of self-discipline, at least in the initial stages before such an approach becomes a more natural part of our lives.

We should hurry less, and consciously curb impatience whilst reflecting more before taking action in any given situation.

17

Keeping Life Simple
Living Life

I was trying to buy some basic items at a store today. A few decades ago, there would not have been any problem at all. Life was simple. Correspondingly, stores were generally small and carried, in the main, just basic items in any event. Times have changed. The sheer number of categories of aisles containing items was itself confusing. After I had located the appropriate aisle, I was bewildered by the vast variety of items themselves. Many of these items were not basic but were "souped-up" in nature; others were simply impractical, in my view, and only intended for those who were intent on indulging themselves over and above their basic needs. To make matters worse, I could only locate one of the items I wanted! And so I had to go to another store – again, a very large one and (not surprisingly) a competitor of the previous one. I was not much more fortunate in the second store, although I did locate a couple of other items. This left me wondering, for this experience was symptomatic of the times, I believe, in which we live.

In the first place (and this is not a new concept at all), we are living in an age of rampant consumerism. Indeed, even as people save scraps of paper in the name of going green, we are deluged with unnecessary flyers and brochures, all seeking our hard earned

money. Instead of offering basic items of good quality, we are deluged with all manner of consumer goods – not all of which are practical to begin with. Ironically, as we pamper ourselves with more and more items, including unnecessary ones, we are becoming an increasingly "throwaway" society – even as many other people around the world suffer because they do not even have the basic necessities of life.

This *attitude* of avoiding simplicity in favour of unnecessary extravagance is not confined to our consumption of consumer goods. It permeates other parts of our lives as well, for example, at the workplace where a lot of time is wasted (I have dealt with this in more detail in another reflection).[14] To take another example, even the celebration of birthdays (and other happy occasions) becomes

---

14 See Reflection 27: The Meaninglessness of 'Busyness' – Yet Further Reflection on Work.

over-elaborate, on occasion at least. However, when this occurs, it often celebrates the giver rather than the person whose special day it is. Put simply, by not keeping things simple, we lose sight of the basic purpose for the occasion concerned. The fact of the matter is that this is not a new point at all – many books have been written, with many elaborating on what is essentially a simple point!

So I will keep this particular reflection short – and simple – and end here.

Keep life simple.

18

Speak Only in Order to Edify and/or Uplift
Speech

Although it sounds clichéd, it was indeed very much the case many decades ago that people from Asian societies (in my case, Singapore society) were much more reticent. Indeed, this was so from my own experience as a university lecturer in the early days of my career. It was quite difficult to get students to speak up on a regular basis at tutorials, even though it was clear that many of them had something to say and/or knew the answer(s) to the questions we were considering.

Such reticence is no longer the case. Whilst I am glad that people are speaking up more, on occasion at least, it is, in my respectful view, overdone. Let me elaborate. Before I do so, perhaps the change in such culture in the Singapore context can be attributed, in part at least, to the increased (and perhaps even increasing) "Westernisation" of Singapore society, which stands very much at the crossroads between East and West (which is, of course, no bad thing in itself).

However, as just alluded to, increased speech today is not always beneficial. Sometimes, it is "empty". Indeed, some people enjoy hearing the sound of their own voices, not realising that, even though others are often too polite to intervene (let alone cut

them short), they are wasting everybody's time. And eloquent, albeit "empty" words do not make the situation any better. Indeed, very early on in my academic career, I realised that, if I did not deliver a sufficiently impactful lecture, I was not wasting just one hour of my own time, but 250 hours in a class of 250 students. Further, it is just plain inconsiderate and rude to drone on if the words uttered are "empty". There is, in fact, another type of "empty" speech: insincere flattery that is effected for a variety of purposes. For example, such speech is often selfish and self-serving, such as when one flatters a superior in order to move up the corporate ladder. Unfortunately, for others, it is just a bad habit of flattering all and sundry. But woe betide them when others discover their insincerity for it can feel quite hurtful. For example, if everyone is said to be excellent, then nobody is excellent at all!

Worse still, there are some people whose speech is positively negative. Whilst it is true that we have all occasionally transgressed by stating negative things when we ought not to, there are people whose general mission in life appears (unfortunately) to be geared towards putting others down through their speech. Indeed, on one occasion, someone even mentioned publicly that one does not have to be substantively better than another person to be considered superior to that person, one need only put him or her down, and one would "automatically" be superior! However, negative (still worse, hateful) speech can actually leave deeper wounds and scars than actual physical blows.

So what, then, should our speech be like, ideally? In my view, the answer is simple. If one has nothing good to say, do not say it. If a person could really do with some wise and constructive criticism, this may be done privately (but only after much reflection, bearing in mind that nobody, including each and every one of us, is perfect). Put simply, such speech must *edify*. However, I would go further – if one has something *positive and good* to say, then it should be said with sincerity. And hence, contrary to an earlier example I gave, if someone truly deserves to be praised, then one should say it sincerely and not overegg the pudding (lest sincere praise turns out to be unintentionally, and uncomfortably, cloying). Only in this way can such speech be *uplifting*. Indeed (and more generally), the *manner* in which our speech is framed is also very important (as is also the case with the previous example centring on edification). One good general rule of thumb is to try one's best to be as *sincere* as possible. Speech is a vital aspect of everyone's lives – let us use it *wisely and sincerely*.

> ***True speech is that which edifies***
> ***and/or uplifts another.***

19

Neither Envying nor Fretting, but Committing Instead

Contentment

What I am going to say might sound idealistic and perhaps even unreal, so let me commence this reflection by relating a real life experience from my time during National Service. I have, in fact, spoken about this in public to illustrate a slightly different point (about commitment to one's professional craft) although, as we shall see below, both this point, as well as the one that is the focus of this reflection (that one should be content with one's lot), are indeed related.

After I had completed my Basic Military Training in the army, I was assigned to be a clerk. I should say that this is not, at first blush, an impressive vocation by any means (especially when viewed from a military perspective). My parents were concerned with my (perceived lack of) dexterity and immediately purchased a portable typewriter for me to practise on! Indeed, there were a few fellow students at the initial clerical course who were less than enthusiastic about their new vocation. I do not know whether it was fear of the threat of being kept back for extra typing practice but I plugged (or should I say typed) on, practising as we were advised by our instructors, even during lunch time (I was often the only one!). It was tough going initially because typing was quite alien to me. However, even without an overt religious perspective at that particular point in time, I was a firm believer in being committed to every task that one was entrusted with. And it was not dependent, in my view, on whether one was gifted at the task that was given and/or whether that task was perceived by others to be important. It was simply a matter of integrity and good conscience.[15]

Now, looking back almost half a century later, I can confirm what I have always believed – there are no coincidences in life and one's worth is not measured by the material wealth and/or status that one possesses. We all have a destiny and nobody is any less worthy than another – *provided that one lives one's life with honesty, integrity and commitment, and is always open to helping others whenever and wherever required.* In my view, this is of the first importance because I know of many people who are so very unhappy with their respective lot in life – many wish that they are more successful and this becomes even sadder when their reach exceeds their grasp. We have all been accorded different abilities as well as gifts in life. Some may not necessarily result in material wealth and/or fame but, in my view at least, one is successful if one is successful at whatever vocation one has been placed in and all the more when one has touched another life, whether in big or small ways, for the better.

I would like to underscore the point that I have just made by sharing a little about my own life. As I plugged away as a clerk in the army, I was sent on more advanced clerical courses. And in the most advanced course I attended (together with army regulars, many of whom were Chief Clerks in their respective units), I even managed to complete a lengthy copy-typing exercise without making a single typographical error. It might sound childish, but I felt quite proud when the instructor displayed my work on the

---

15 See also Reflection 10: Always Do the Right Thing – Integrity, and Reflection 11: Do Your Best, Regardless … – True Excellence.

class noticeboard for all to see. More pragmatically, I knew then that I had a skill that could earn me a living, if necessary. If all I was destined to be was a typist, then I knew that I would try to be the best typist I could be. Little did I know then that there were other skill sets that I had yet to unearth.

Learning to type quickly and accurately would later stand me in good stead when I embarked on my doctoral thesis. More importantly, that same work ethic and commitment would also stand me in good stead not only in law school but also in my later professional career, first as a legal academic and then as a judge. As is often said, hindsight is 20/20 vision, but all I can say is that had I planned my life, I could not have planned it any better. On a personal level, there was clearly divine providence as well as provision. However, I know that I had to do my part as well. Looking back now, it is clear that being *content* with what I had and not envying others as well as fretting about what I did not have was an attitude that always furnished me with the necessary peace of mind. As it turned out, nothing was wasted. Indeed, I was blessed with success that I could not ever have imagined as a shy soldier in the army. Even more than professional success, I have a wonderful family. I am so thankful and have no regrets whatsoever.

Be neither envious of others nor worry about what you do not have. Instead, be content. Treasure what you have and utilise what abilities and gifts that have been given to you to the fullest, helping others along the way whenever and wherever appropriate.

20

Beneficial 'Forgetfulness'
Handling Injustice

I would be hugely surprised if anyone said that they had never suffered any injustice whatsoever throughout their lives. I would be equally surprised if they said that they did not – on occasion at least – feel like taking matters into their own hands and seeking some kind of recompense or even revenge. The fact of the matter is that, at one time or another and to a lesser or greater extent, we have all suffered injustice. Some injustice is so severe that the persons concerned might even lose their life or liberty. Most of us can be grateful for the fact that we have not had to endure such severe injustice.

I will freely admit that I have suffered injustice on a great many occasions in my life. Most people who know me only focus on the positive things that have happened in my life and are unaware that I have gone through several experiences of injustice – a few of which, had they occurred to the fullest extent possible, might have irreparably damaged me and/or ruined my career. In fairness, some of the objectionable conduct was not intentional and stemmed from insensitivity. Be that as it may, objectively speaking, the harm caused to me was substantial all the same.

The standard advice one receives is that one should not be "bitter" about such experiences so that one can become "better".

Please do not misunderstand – I think this is excellent advice. The problem, speaking personally at least, is that, like most things in life, this advice is easier to state than to practise. Indeed, it is always easier to give advice to someone suffering from injustice when one is in a state of relative equilibrium. There is itself a lesson in this, I think, but I digress. To return to the topic at hand, I think that there is much to be learnt from the standard advice, provided that one is prepared to put it into *practice*. In this regard, I have learnt that a substantial – or even giant – step towards handling injustice is what I would term "forgetfulness". You see, experiencing injustice is like suffering a serious wound. Dwelling on the injustice one has suffered – and, even worse, being bitter about it – is like allowing the wound to fester. It may even become septic and thereafter poison one's entire system. The end result is a profoundly damaged person – one who is far more damaged than even the original injustice warrants.

It seems to me that "forgetfulness" is a counterpoint to the danger of festering I have just mentioned. It is not "denial", although there is, admittedly, a fine line between "forgetfulness" and "denial". What I have in mind regarding the former is this: that one let go (as best as one can under the circumstances) of the effects of the injustice suffered and that means moving forward with one's life rather than dwelling unhealthily on the injustice suffered. It is true that we are all human and so spending some time dwelling on the injustice is inevitable. However, I have found that the trick is not to dwell *too* long on it. Life on this side of eternity is too short. I was, in fact, amazed how very effective or beneficial such "forgetfulness" is. Let me elaborate with a short story of my own.

When I was both lecturing as well as writing my doctorate thesis, I was, literally, "drowning". In fact, the harder I tried, the harder things became. Hence, any encouragement I received was worth more than its weight in gold. Unfortunately, the discouragement outweighed the encouragement. It was all the more dispiriting when the source of discouragement emanated from persons who ought to have encouraged me instead. I will not dwell on the details as it is, in my view, unedifying to do so. However, for the purposes of this reflection, it was a revelation of sorts when I met my former lecturer during a stint on sabbatical leave overseas. He was a wonderful teacher and a great mentor. We had not met for many years. As we reminisced about our time at the university (he as a lecturer and I as a student and, later, lecturer), I recounted my terrible experience of teaching as well as writing my doctoral thesis at the same time. This was when he recounted a particular occasion when a really unkind remark was made to me when I mentioned that I needed a slight reduction in my workload as I was "drowning".

I must confess that I could not immediately recall that occasion. It was only after "trawling" through my memories that I ultimately recalled what had happened. I should add that I do not generally have a bad memory by any means. So what had happened? I can sincerely say that I had not pushed this horrible experience into the inner recesses of my consciousness by way of denial. I then recalled that what I had done was to forget about the injustice that had been done to me. I had so much to do that bitterness and self-pity were not particularly practical options at the time. The fact of the matter is that I had somehow forgotten (almost) completely about this terrible experience over the years. And by doing so, the wound did not fester; it had healed instead (all without further conscious effort on my part). And you know something? As I remembered this occasion, I no longer felt any anger or animosity towards the person who had perpetrated this injustice upon me. At that moment, I felt really free – indeed, I had already freed myself many years ago but I had only then come to realise what had actually happened.

I would like to conclude by stating that it is *extremely* difficult to practise what I have termed "beneficial 'forgetfulness'" in the ordinary course of life. This is where having *spiritual* help is, in my view, essential. Indeed, I would go so far to state that, as a young Christian at the time of the recounted event, I was (unbeknownst to myself at the time) being helped so that I could forgive my enemy – even if love for that enemy (as taught by the Bible) was not forthcoming. Having said this, I think that the principle of "beneficial 'forgetfulness'" is *still* relevant even if one does not believe in God and wants to move on with one's life in spite of the injustice one has suffered. Perhaps one may not (even as a Christian) forgive, but one can always forget. And that is a useful first step, if nothing else.

A good first step in handling injustice to oneself is to forget about the injustice lest it festers and destroys you, and the next step is to not only forget but to forgive as well.

21

A Shattered Cup Can be Mended
Adversity

There are some images that stay with one for a lifetime. One of these came from a former colleague whose profound scepticism was not only troubling but also gave me lots of food for thought. In particular, he was sceptical of anything to do with religion, and that led to a comment he made on yet another colleague, asserting that the other colleague was like a shattered cup that could not possibly be mended and that the other person's religious beliefs were just an illusion after all. If, however, he was correct, then there would be no hope for virtually everyone, including himself. The fact of the matter is that the world is imperfect. Indeed, I recall that when I was young, the news was much more mixed, there would be both good news as well as bad. In the space of a few decades, things have changed radically. Most of the news we receive nowadays is (unfortunately) bad news – even tragic news. More to the point, even in the less dramatic contexts of our own lives, we have to accept that life is far from perfect and that there will be many difficulties along our life's path. Indeed, acknowledging that life is not perfect is, in my view, an important first step. Unbeknownst to myself, I used to harbour a very strong perfectionist streak. The trouble was that it was not obvious and, to make matters worse, I would often

rationalise it away by stating that life was not perfect. However, that resulted in a contradiction that could – and did – lead to much unintended pain. I hasten to add, though, that the other extreme in approach did not – and does not – appeal to me either: that we should just give up on the basis that the world is so imperfect that there is nothing that can be done about it.

A *balanced* approach is required. Coming back to my former colleague's observation which I referred to at the start of this reflection, I should say that I do not believe that religion (and the supernatural) is a farce and a crutch. I should also say that, in some (albeit not all) cases, miracles do happen and, in those cases, a shattered cup *can be made perfectly whole again*. However, even if we leave religion aside for the moment, my own view is embodied in that old adage that "where there is life, there is hope". In this regard, even a shattered cup can be mended. It might not – absent a miracle – be perfectly whole again, but it (and its pieces) need not (and ought not) be cast aside. Such an attitude requires *hope* – and, in particular, hope in people and their ability to restore to themselves at least some of what has been lost in the situation concerned. Any other attitude would lead to despair and, indeed, that happens all too often for comfort.

However, as with most things in life, all this is mere "theory" until we *practise* it and thereby *confirm its reality from our own experience*. And, to that extent, I can only exhort you, dear reader, to try this attitude out for yourself. However, I am willing to state that, should you do so, you will never regret it. Your cup may not be completely mended, but you will be sufficiently mended to know that it is worthwhile to help others mend themselves and that, in time, this will set in motion a "chain reaction" that will confirm that "where there is life, there is hope". Indeed, your cup might even become more beautiful. In the Japanese art of *kintsugi*, broken pottery is mended with lacquer mixed with powdered gold or other precious metals such as silver or platinum, resulting in a more beautiful piece of art that simultaneously displays the history of that piece itself.

Never underestimate the power of hope.

22

Do Not Despair, and Continue to Live Life Meaningfully
An Imperfect World

Even taking into account the more archaic state of communications and technology back in the day, I remember my time during childhood to be less fraught with bad news. That having been said, the world is – even at the best of times – an imperfect place. There had already been two world wars even before I was born. Perhaps it is a very human response not to think about the terrible state the world is in (and, especially, the inhumanity often practised on individuals or even at a societal level). And, as if this was not bad enough, we all face one inexorable enemy (and related end) on this side of eternity – physical death. Indeed, for those who believe that all that exists now in the physical world is all we are, have and can be, the situation might be even worse.

All this was driven home in a much more personal way this past weekend. I follow association football quite closely. It does take up an awful lot of time but it has been a hobby (and possibly "addiction"!) for almost half a century of my life. Without even consciously learning about the sport, I am quite steeped in it and am interested in every aspect of it. And so, when a tragic accident occurred this past week which resulted in the death of an owner of a football club, this could not be ignored – a point driven home by the fact that he was the same age as I am. A former manager of the English national team also nearly lost his life through a heart attack this very same weekend – and he is also the same age as I am. Then, the very next day, news comes in from the wider world of an airline disaster that probably took the lives of all the 189 who were on board that plane.

What, then, are we to do in the face of such stark, and often tragic, reality? This also raises – for some people at least – all sorts of other (and larger) questions such as the very meaning of life itself. I do not – and cannot – come even remotely close to proposing a clear solution (particularly in a short reflection such as this). However, I felt compelled to write this reflection to at least clarify my own philosophy and approach towards this specific issue.

It is perhaps useful to commence with the very real fact that injustice and suffering are an inevitable part of what is a fundamentally imperfect world. However, mere acceptance of this fact does not, in my view, necessarily entail a pessimistic (let alone fatalistic) attitude. Neither does it entail a selfish attitude either, where the satisfaction of one's own desires takes pride of place simply because a selfish life is meaningless – except to the extent, perhaps, that one believes that this physical existence is all that there is. However, even if this last-mentioned point were correct, living a life full of self would not negate its *ultimate* meaninglessness since, by definition, there would be nothing beyond this physical life. Still less should we become cynical as well as sceptical for, if nothing else, we will poison ourselves in the process.

This brings me to a fundamental point which I have touched on in another reflection – that there is *true* meaning in life when we impact *other* lives for *the better*.[16] Even for those who do not believe that there is life beyond this physical life, impacting other

---

16 See, for example, Reflection 35: Looking Beyond Ourselves, and Reflection 36: Like Candles Burning Brightly – Living a Meaningful Life.

lives for the better means that we have imparted a *legacy* through our actions – a legacy that could, hopefully, become a *living* one that impacts *yet other* lives, perhaps even *after* our relatively brief sojourn on this earth has ended if others whom we have impacted for the better pay this forward by helping others in turn. That is why, in my view, we should not despair over the imperfection in this world and the obvious injustice as well as suffering that results, although the sheer volume of the injustice and suffering can be so very discouraging at times. While what we can accomplish may appear relatively small, we should never underestimate the impact of our actions (as briefly alluded to above).

> *Although we live in an imperfect world,*
> *we should not despair but should, instead,*
> *continue to live life as meaningfully as*
> *we can, impacting other lives for the*
> *better in the process.*

WORK, SERVICE AND REST

23

Of Cleaners, Locksmiths and Calling
Work

"What is the purpose of work?" This seemingly innocuous question belies a multitude of different issues, including the ultimate question as to what constitutes the meaning of our respective lives themselves. Indeed, we spend so very much time at work that it is imperative to give some serious consideration as to what role it plays in our lives.

I must confess that I thought I had resolved this issue for myself many years ago. However, when I began to write this reflection, I found that I had been most mistaken. Ascertaining the purpose of work is far from easy – and rendered even more complicated by the fact that each one of us is so very different.

The traditional approach to work is to view it, first, as a means for survival – to obtain the financial resource to support ourselves and our families. There is, of course, nothing wrong with that. On the contrary, it is both logical as well as commonsensical. However, it does raise the yet *further* question as to why we desire to survive in the first place (in addition to the fact that this appears to be a sensible, indeed visceral, instinct to possess). And this brings us back to the much larger question as to *the meaning of life* itself. Viewed in this light, the purpose of work is connected to the larger question as to the meaning of life.

Another observation I would make is that the above point – that the purpose of work is somehow connected to the larger question of our own meaning in life – may, in fact, prompt different responses towards work itself. Some people never really bother about reflecting on this particular issue, appearing to be in a "neutral zone" and just surviving from day to day. Others are ambitious, indeed, far, far more ambitious: they view work as a means of climbing up the corporate ladder rather than to help others in need. Such an attitude views work as a means of accumulating wealth and enhancing one's status – thus achieving the opportunity to have a significant say over other people's lives. There is yet a third response towards work that overlaps with the preceding two: working mindlessly, without meaning and direction. This will, in fact, be the focus of another reflection.[17] For the present reflection, I must confess that I feel rather helpless attempting to write it – for what could I possibly say about the ultimate meaning of life itself? However, I hope to persuade you, dear reader, that there is at least a part which work can play in helping us to understand the ultimate meaning of life itself. And this thought was confirmed by a couple of my own working life experiences. There are, in fact, others which are also relevant but, for present purposes, the following two will suffice.

The first relates to advice I have often given to new employees at my workplace: that we must always treat everyone, *regardless* of their rank or status in the organisation, with *equal respect*. Indeed, I shared that we are all, in fact, inextricably connected at the workplace such that the proper performance of each person's work (*regardless* of what it is precisely) is important and the opposite (poor performance) can adversely affect our own work. The illustration I often give is the work of our office cleaners. Theirs is a difficult life but the regular cleaners who service the

---

17 See Reflection 27: The Meaninglessness of 'Busyness' – Yet Further Reflection on Work.

vicinity of my office have always carried out their duties both efficiently as well as cheerfully. And I value them as much as I value my other co-workers, not least because it occurred to me one day that if, for some reason, they were unable to do their work, our office environment would become extremely unpleasant, to say the least. Beyond a certain point, coming to the office would pose a physical hazard to our health.

My second illustration was prompted by a very recent experience. Whilst I was in my bedroom, I discovered, as I tried to open the door, that the locking mechanism in the door knob was not functioning. I could not open the door and was literally a "prisoner" in my bedroom! To make matters worse, this occurred in the dead of night. Fortunately, we were able to contact a locksmith, whose work was so professional and satisfactory that I later arranged for him to change *all* the door knobs for the rooms in my home (which were quite old and had therefore led to the malfunction in my bedroom door knob). As I was chatting with him after being "released", he made an observation which I found to be rather striking. The gist of his point was that being a locksmith who worked all hours to help in emergencies (such as the one I had just experienced) was not glamorous work and that few in the younger generation wanted to learn the trade. Yet, like cleaners, what would our lives be like if such professions were to go into serious decline? Indeed, it had been absolutely essential to my welfare as well as peace of mind that I found a reliable locksmith that night who could, literally, release me from my dilemma.

The simple – and more general – lesson is that *all* work is worthy and therefore important. In a related vein, it is therefore imperative that we treat our work as a *vocation* (and, perhaps, even a *calling*) and not merely as an uninteresting means of earning a living. Viewed in this perspective, our work (again, *regardless* of how *the world* values it) furnishes in part, or even a large part, *meaning* to our *lives because, when it is carried out effectively, it will* **impact other lives for the better.** And, as my two illustrations demonstrate (and there are, in fact, more I could have raised), this is clearly the case simply because we are not superhuman and, in any event, cannot humanly cope with every need as well as emergency which we encounter in our lives. And that is also how I have always viewed my work in the different jobs I have had over the last few decades.

All work is worthy because, if performed
well, it impacts lives for the better.

24

Serving Like a Fool

Service

I must confess that I have a problem. Although I know that one should serve others sacrificially without expectation of reward, I am not quite there yet. I think that I have progressed some way along the journey to the extent that as I *do* serve (most of the time at least) without expectation of reward and with the ideal of service as a calling in mind. In this last-mentioned regard, I think that, as far as one's work is concerned, regardless of how pleasant or unpleasant it is, it ought – at any given point in time – be viewed as a calling (as opposed to being merely for survival, although that is a not insignificant benefit as well). Alas, I still, however, have some way to go. Let me explain.

Much as I have grown accustomed to the attitude that one should not expect any reward or return for what one does for others, it still bothers me when I am, instead, "repaid" with offence as well. This is quite human, I guess. Indeed, I know, unfortunately, of many who serve only (or at least primarily) with reward in mind. Whilst I can accept such an attitude, I do not subscribe to it and wish that such people would not characterise their work as "service" simply because it is, at its highest, *self*-serving (which is not what "service", at least as I understand it, is supposed to mean). However, returning to my earlier point, it is thoroughly disappointing, to say the least, when I am (crudely put) "stabbed in the back" by the very person I have assisted. Fortunately, this does not happen too often and I should hasten to add that, on other (more joyous) occasions, I have even been thanked and/or helped as well. On even more joyous occasions, I have also been helped without having done anything for the other person in the first place.

I suffer from a yet further weakness that smacks of hypocrisy on my part. If, as I believe, one should not expect any reward or return for helping others, then why do I occasionally feel upset when I am not thanked for what I have done? This is especially the case when I have done what I felt was something significant for individuals and/or an organisation. There is, admittedly, no small amount of hypocrisy in this – even if basic human decency dictates that some form of thanks is owed. Again, I can put this down to being human. But this is no excuse, because I do think that the ideal embodied in the concept of service must necessarily (as a point of basic principle) entail *sacrifice* on one's part. If this is the case, then it does entail a certain *attitude*, which I would term "being willing to serve like a fool". Indeed, the rest of the world (and, alas, on occasion, even the recipient of one's help) might consider us "fools". If, however, we are willing to embrace as well as live out that attitude, then we will have no regrets. Indeed, I truly believe that, when our work is finally done, we can have peace and be glad that we did our very best, *regardless* of circumstances as well as response. *Put simply, we did our best and did what was right.*

However, as alluded to above, this is no easy task. As also mentioned, I am still learning myself. I believe that such an attitude of service not only does not materialise overnight, but is, on the contrary, a process in the journey of life-long learning.

It also requires great patience and perhaps even greater humility. Despite many disappointments, I am determined to persevere.

True service is helping others without expectation of material reward.

25

How are You?

Meaning of Appreciation and Recognition

I recently began a speech honouring an esteemed colleague on his retirement by stating that it was a little-known fact that I was almost invariably at the back of queues as I tended to let others go ahead first, but that particular occasion was one when I would have made an exception and was more than happy to be at the front of the queue to deliver my tribute. I did also state that this was due to my upbringing, in particular, that I was taught by my parents that I should always be polite and not rush. Whilst this is true, I could not help but reflect, on occasion, how this posture of diffidence was strangely juxtaposed with my diligence. Regardless of how others perceive the results of my efforts, in whatever I do, I attempt my level best to maintain (for the most part at least) the utmost effort and diligence in the task that has been assigned to me. However, on many occasions, the posture of diffidence has meant that I did not receive the full credit that my efforts deserved. I nevertheless do – and continue to – persevere for, as I have written in the previous reflection on service, true service is helping others without expectation of reward.[18] However, I am only human and there is, even on a logical level, a certain injustice when others take credit for the work one does. Viewed in this light, the present reflection

---

18 See Reflection 24: Serving Like a Fool – Service.

is a continuation of the previous one and attempts to grapple with the all-too-human desire to be recognised for the effort one puts in.

Indeed, I often (half) joke with others that this is the story of my life – the fact (as I often put it) that I always draw the short straw (which was literally true on at least one occasion, but that is perhaps another story for another time). What I *do* mean is that I do not always receive the recognition that I expect or that I think I deserve.

I must confess that much of the (negative) feelings are due more to human ego and pride and, in that regard, there is no justification whatsoever for such an attitude. However, there is a more nuanced reason why such recognition constitutes unnecessary baggage in one's personal life in the final analysis. I was reminded of this when my family and I had moved some years back. I had carefully packed my various medals and prizes in a box (they were all *individually* attained consistently with what I have already mentioned in the earlier part of this reflection). However, when I opened the box, I was startled. Not surprisingly, in the process of moving, all the medals and prizes in the box got jumbled together and what greeted my eyes was not a very pleasant sight – to put in plainly, at first sight, if I were an objective third party, the items would have appeared like junk to me. In one sense, they were, because it was what *underlay* them that counted and which would continue to survive in my memory even if the medals and prizes had been lost or destroyed in transit, and this related to the effort I had put into the various activities and the sense of achievement and, more importantly, the lessons that I had learnt along the way. But one can take this principle one step further, in my view – the absence of *material* recognition does *not diminish* either the efforts or the result of those efforts and *those* are what count in the final analysis.[19]

---

19 See further a fuller elaboration of this particular episode in Reflection 28: Jumbled Medals – Meaning of Success.

And just recently as well as a few days before, I was approached by graduates from a former hall of residence where I had served for some years as a resident fellow, simply to greet me and to ask how I was. I was amazed that they could still recognise me after well over two decades and still more amazed that they would think to approach me. I was also reminded that this was not the only time that such an occurrence had happened and that former students of mine have also approached me over the years, long after their graduation. I was then further reminded of the cards and letters of appreciation that I have received over the years. What left me reflecting anew in a radical fashion was the fact that, despite my perception that my efforts had not been appreciated, in point of fact, I was being obsessed with *formal (and often "official" or "bureaucratic") recognition (that invariably takes the form of material or physical awards) – whereas the **true** recognition as well as appreciation had been accorded to me all along, although (shamefully, I must say) I never recognised it in as holistic a manner as I ought to have.* And, almost as if to underscore the point, I was finally reminded that I was, in fact, given a material or physical award – albeit from a student alumni association which honoured a couple of lecturers, including myself, whom they truly appreciated. It also happened to be the case, in my view at least (and certainly for myself!), that the official organisation had not really recognised our efforts in such a significant manner at all.

All this taught me new lessons – amongst other things, that we should not be quick to overlook *true* appreciation just because it does not manifest itself in a *formal* way and that we should, in any event, recognise that the formal symbols of recognition are not valuable in themselves. And that brings me – full circle, as it were – to my other reflection on service: that we ought to serve simply *because that is the good and right thing to do* and that, in thus serving, we must simultaneously be prepared to not only persevere but also to sacrifice. Any appreciation and recognition that we may receive are mere "bonuses".

We must never forget that true appreciation and recognition can, and often do, take many forms, but they are mere "bonuses" for we serve because true service is helping others without expectation of reward.

26

A Happy Worker is an Effective Worker

Further Reflection on Work

Work – now, more than ever before – dominates our lives. That is, of course, not necessarily a good thing at all. I have attempted to deal with some of the negative aspects of such a phenomenon in another reflection.[20] I want now to deal briefly with what are, in substance, interpersonal relationships within the workplace itself. In this regard, it is quite disconcerting, personally, to have people agree with me (more often than not) that politics is a given in the workplace. Indeed, many years ago, a pastor whom my wife and I greatly respect surprised us by stating that where there is more than one person, there will be politics. The reasons for the (petty) politics we find at the workplace are various. Many centre on the need to climb up the corporate ladder not through (at least only) hard work but through what has been termed "managing upwards" as well. But what this normally means is that fellow employees at the same level or at level(s) below are not treated with respect and may even be manipulated and/or cheated. That this is done with a veneer of courtesy is, in my view, particular perturbing. One can

---

20 See Reflection 27: The Meaninglessness of 'Busyness' – Yet Further Reflection on Work.

argue that this is only human nature, which is not unpersuasive. However, unless we can rise above our baser instincts of pride and selfishness, we are not going to be happy workers. The irony is that we might become materially rich workers but there will never be happiness in the form of true peace and contentment that is, in my view, really essential to fulfilment at the workplace. Indeed, such conduct results in a *double*-detriment – not only is the victim of politics unhappy but the perpetrator himself or herself will, as just mentioned, also not find *true* happiness.

There is another trend at the workplace which I also find rather disturbing and is not unrelated to the first which I have briefly talked about. Indeed, it is probably related to the first in that it is also rooted in the basic approach of selfishness. More to the point, this relates to the inability to be generous or to show kindness at the workplace. I have, in fact, touched on the importance of little kindnesses in another reflection.[21] However, whether big or small, kindnesses shown at the workplace make for a much happier environment all round. Indeed, it is often the case that a little kindness can mean so very much to a fellow employee when he or she is already under an enormous amount of stress. That little kindness may even avert the straw that might break the proverbial camel's back in the life of the person concerned.

Such an attitude is perhaps even more important for bosses to practise. Instead of squeezing the last ounce of work from a subordinate (I have also dealt with this in another reflection),[22] being empathetic and generous can, ironically, actually result in a *more productive* employee because I have found, in my own experience, that a happy employee tends to be a more effective employee as well. Contrary to the sceptic's view, people do generally respond to kindness positively. This is especially so

---

21 See Reflection 7: Little Kindnesses – Power of Kindnes
22 See Reflection 1: No Crushed Sugar Cane – How to Treat Others.

because, even in my own limited experience, I have witnessed a lot of mean-spiritedness being demonstrated for no apparent reason at all. There is, of course, the potential danger that an employee who is shown kindness might *take advantage* of such kindness – by taking such kindness for weakness. All I would say is that it is worth taking that risk rather than adopting a blanket approach in the opposite direction. I would add that if an employee truly takes advantage of the kindness shown to him or her, then the boss concerned should also exercise the wisdom to respond accordingly.

In short, if one can do one's part to eradicate the scourge of petty politics from the workplace whilst simultaneously demonstrating kindness whenever possible, everyone concerned would be much happier and, as importantly, be more effective in their work.

Sincerity and kindness at the workplace will benefit both giver and receiver alike.

27

The Meaninglessness of 'Busyness'
Yet Further Reflection on Work

As I sat down to write this reflection, I realised that its thrust ran counter to what appears to be the conventional "wisdom" towards this subject in the world today. This centres on the concept of "busyness" and its role in our working life. Many decades ago (and when I was much younger!), life, as they say, was much simpler, and this included work as well. The traditional "9 to 5" job was very much a central motif of working life, regardless of the job concerned. Indeed, the more immediate problem – at least in the Singapore context of yesteryear – was to be able to find a job in the first place. In this regard, people were also much less fussy about their jobs. It was simply a matter of feeding the family first – anything else beyond survival was a bonus. However, my sense was that, despite this, people were all much happier. It was almost certainly the case as far as working life was concerned. Yes, there were the usual grouses about bosses and/or colleagues (which just goes to show that nothing changes where human nature is concerned!). However, there was not that deep-seated feeling of intense busyness as well as the immense stress (and probably illnesses) that accompanied it.

Much has changed in the intervening decades. I have felt it in a very tangible way myself. Indeed, when I first started working life, I do not recall feeling as stressed as I began to become in the decades since. And this is even making the allowance for the fact that I was in an academic job. In point of fact, academia nowadays appears to be so much more stressful. Might I suggest that this is just a symptom of a wider societal development (or, perhaps more accurately, a step *backwards*). It is almost a *badge of honour* to emphasise how *busy* one is. And those of us who wish to adopt a more sensible approach towards working life cannot avoid busyness either because those who *wish to be* busy make all of us busy as well! I do not think that I am being facetious. It is, of course, true that things cannot always remain the same and that with, for example, the advent of technology, we are *necessarily* busier. And make no mistake about it – *diligence and hard work are necessary*. However, my point is simply this – even allowing for developments such as that just mentioned, is it *really necessary* to be *as busy* as most of us find ourselves at the present time?

In my view, the answer is that it is *not* necessary. Let me elaborate with a thought experiment (which I actually hope will be experimented with by you, dear reader, in real life). Imagine, first, that you went about your work with one cardinal principle in mind, which is *not to waste time*. That would, I suggest, have very significant consequences. For one thing, it would mean that we would not have to spend so much time attempting to impress others, including our bosses – except to the extent that our *actual work* might accomplish that. That would mean going *directly to the point* – "prettifying" our work and *appearing* to be busy for its own sake, for example, would go out of the window. And for those of us for whom it is our job to establish committees and to hold meetings, to take another example, this would mean cutting down on committees (and, of course, sub-committees and sub-sub-committees established so that bosses at each level could be impressed!) and, of course, on actual meetings themselves.

It is notoriously clear that many meetings take an inordinately long time because of persons who (if I may put it plainly) love to speak simply for the pleasure of hearing their own voices in public. What is worse is that, as a result, nothing of note often gets *decided* at the end of these lengthy meetings. Imagine, again, that you wanted to *focus* on getting your job done. In this regard, we all know that the shortest distance between two points is a straight line and that if one's ruler is not defective, one should be able to connect those two points fairly quickly. Put simply, the *quality* of our work is as, if not more, important than the *quantity* of time we put into it. This is *not* to suggest in any way that we should not put in the *requisite* time and effort into our work, but it does no good (and, on the contrary, results in great harm) to our minds and bodies when we simply put in *quantities* of time *for their own sake*.

I could go on, but I will stop here because I think there is already sufficient food for thought. Put simply, mere "busyness" for its own sake is meaningless and may, in fact, be clearly detrimental to our mental and/or physical health. We need, in other words, to "work smart". And this also means working with honesty and integrity, putting in our best efforts into each piece of work. However, what we do need to avoid is – to reiterate the point – "busyness" for its own sake.

While diligence and hard work are necessary, busyness at work for its own sake is meaningless. We should, instead, always focus on the substance of our tasks and aim to complete them as efficiently and effectively as possible.

28

Jumbled Medals
Meaning of Success

In a previous reflection, I concluded that true success is when we impact, in both large and small ways, the lives of others for the better.[23] However, I feel compelled to return to this topic (that is, the meaning of success or, rather, *true* success). This is, in the main, because for all the rhetoric to the contrary that we often hear, the reality is quite different. Put simply, there is a clear *disconnect* between principle on the one hand and practical action on the other. There remains a preoccupation – even an obsession – with *material* success (without which one is presumed by large sectors of society to matter little, or not at all). And this reminds me of a story concerning me – it is a story of "jumbled medals". Let me elaborate.

Many years ago, as my family and I were preparing to move house (and many will tell you that the stress of moving is enormous, some say it is second only to losing a loved one), amidst the hustle and bustle of packing, I made sure that my medals (mainly my school swimming medals) were packed neatly into a separate and distinct box, which then taped up carefully and transported very gingerly to our new home. Why the fuss, one might legitimately ask? You see, when I was in

23 See Reflection 23: Of Cleaners, Locksmiths and Calling – Work.

secondary school, my parents thought it would be best if I took up swimming as a sport. Being well-intentioned, they thought that it would assist me when I went into the army for National Service. It is true that swimming developed my fitness and stamina to a large extent, although it concerned (unfortunately) a different set of muscles as far as the army was concerned (but that is a point that need not concern us here). I should add that I had *learnt how to swim* only fairly recently before taking it up as a sport. Not surprisingly, I began training from the bottom of the proverbial ladder. It was a real struggle. Being rather less able at least at the beginning, the coaches entered me in events which very few swimmers would enter: the long-distance events.

The good part is that it did develop my fitness as well as stamina (which did, in fact, help me in my army training), as well as an ability to be doggedly persistent (one had to be, in order to just finish the race to begin with).

It took me quite some time to win my very first medal. It was only a bronze medal. However, as a breakthrough prize, it meant the world to me. I still recall being so very upset when sometime later, the medal contrived to detach itself from its wooden plaque. Fortunately, my dear father helped to glue it back for me. After some years, I finally got into my school swimming team. That was another great milestone for me because my school had the best swimming team at that time and it was notoriously difficult to get into the team. You can imagine my delight when I finally won my first gold medal. And so all the medals went into the mentioned box. When I gingerly opened the box on arrival at our new home, however, I was shocked – despite the care I took in transporting them, they were all jumbled up as a result of the car ride and what greeted my eyes were not neatly placed mementos of my previous sporting success (there was also one academic medal as well, by the way) but a box of what looked like, at first glance at least, a pile of miscellaneous things (to another observer not in the know, he or she might have termed it less politely as "junk").

One thought immediately coursed through my mind then and it has stayed with me ever since – the material trappings of success are merely symbolic and do not mean anything in and of themselves. It took a box of jumbled medals to remind me of this very real truth. The truth of the matter, in my case at least, was that this reminded me of what lay behind the medals, which included the perseverance that was needed and how much humility was required in order to obtain them. It also reminded me that a nostalgic attitude towards past achievements, whilst not unwarranted on occasion, is meaningless to the extent that it does not assist us in impacting, in both large and small ways, the lives of others for the better.

By way of a postscript, whilst the medals were, in fact, ultimately placed neatly on a shelf, recent examination of some of them revealed much deterioration. Perhaps this is only to be expected after well over four decades, and it further drives home the message of this reflection.

The material trappings of success do not mean anything in and of themselves save to the extent that they remind us to be humble and to impact, in both large and small ways, the lives of others for the better.

29

Mountain Top or Mountain Help?

Further Reflection on Meaning of Success

In another reflection,[24] I begin by stating that we live in a materially driven society and concluded that so long as we learn from our failures in life and persevere without giving up, that is indeed true "success". And I *added* in the final sentence of that particular reflection that when we truly impact *other lives* for the *better* (and *not necessarily* only in *material* terms), that might well *also* be said to be true "success". Indeed, I want, in this reflection, to elaborate upon this as it also overlaps with what I had stated in yet another reflection on the meaning of work.[25] This is particularly important in view of the continued perception that it is only *material* success that counts. It is understandable why material success ranks so highly in our society. First, it accords with human nature which, in its original and unrestrained form, boils down to individual selfishness and vanity. Secondly, material success is easy to ascertain precisely because of its very nature – it is base and crude, and therefore easy to record. Thirdly (and this is linked to the first point), it often confers (again in a rather base and crude manner) influence and even power over others. A moment's reflection will reveal,

---

24 See Reflection 31: The Failure of 'Failure' – Yet Further Reflection on Meaning of Success.
25 See Reflection 23: Of Cleaners, Locksmiths and Calling – Work.

once again, that the view that material success is the only success is one that may justifiably be characterised as simplistic, pathetic as well as incredibly impoverished.

But what, then, about the *other* view which I have advocated – that true "success" occurs when one truly impacts other lives for the better (and not necessarily in material terms)? It is, in fact, the very *antithesis* of the materialistic approach. First, it militates against the baser human nature and demands that we transcend that with, amongst other things, the qualities of humility and compassion in order that we might minister in both large and small ways to others in need (whether material or, more often than not, otherwise). Secondly, unlike the materialistic approach, it is almost impossible to quantify and ascertain; indeed, because it can, as mentioned, take the form of both significant as well as (seemingly) insignificant forms, one cannot (except in the rare or exceptional case) know with any certainty what the impact of one's actions is. However, at this juncture, I should emphasise that substance here trumps form – put simply (and as elaborated upon in my reflection on the meaning of work[26]), even the seemingly smallest of gestures might, unbeknownst to us, have a life-changing impact on another individual. It is true that all this requires a certain amount of "faith". Thirdly, adopting the approach I have advocated does not only *not* confer influence or power over others but also has, in fact, the *opposite* effect – it requires, as already alluded to, a posture of humility and compassion.

Perhaps I can liken what I have stated to the following illustration. Scaling as well as conquering mountains, especially formidable ones such as Mount Everest, is generally perceived as being a great (even monumental) achievement. Why is that so? Does the achievement lie in the *literal* act of reaching the peak (or,

---

26 See Reflection 23: Of Cleaners, Locksmiths and Calling – Work.

on the materialistic approach, having one's bank account filled to overflowing) – perhaps even by relying on the efforts of others to carry one's supplies up the mountain top in the process? Or does it lie, instead, in the *process* of scaling the mountain itself, during which one learns discipline and endurance, *and* may even be able to help *others* who are less able and who may find themselves stranded in the process, becoming potential victims to exposure and even death on the mountainside? I think that the former is far less fulfilling and is akin to rushing up as well as reaching an empty mountaintop – a result that is devoid of significance, save to the extent (on the other approach) that one has managed to help fellow climbers along the way. The choice is, of course, ours.

True success is when we impact,
in both large and small ways,
the lives of others for the better.

30

Rest for Life
Sleep

It is an almost inevitable fact of life that, generally speaking, we are getting less and less sleep. The busyness of life in general and work in particular constitute part of the many causes for such an unfortunate state of affairs. There is also the lure of technology as many of us spend more and more time on our technological gadgets – in particular, surfing the Internet – until the wee hours of the morning. However, recent studies have demonstrated something which is, in fact, self-evident as well as commonsensical – that if we are sleep-deprived, we not only function less efficiently the next day, but more importantly, we are doing great damage to our bodies, both physically as well as mentally. And such damage might – and often does – have a long term impact on our overall health, visiting us with a vengeance in the future.

Yet, to many, being able to stay awake until the wee hours of the morning gives a false sense of security. Amongst other things, there is the common perception that one can do more and thereby gain an advantage over colleagues if one stays up late (especially to meet deadlines from bosses). For many, though, this is illusory because the *quality* of one's work might in fact suffer. But, then again, there is the perception on the other side of the fence, so to speak – the perception that others might have of one's diligence.

Again, this says nothing of possibly lowering the quality of one's work in point of fact as well as the (even irreparable) damage that is done to our bodies and mind.

We all require sleep in order to enable our bodies and minds to repair as well as rejuvenate themselves. The quantity of sleep required by each person will obviously differ. On a personal level, I have found that I can in fact function fairly well with less sleep than the average person. I used to think that it was not only a gift but a very valuable one at that – for all the reasons stated above. However, I also always knew that I was nevertheless punishing myself unnecessarily. It is true – as I have alluded to above – that the negative effects were not as obvious when I was younger. However, with age (and a correspondingly heavier workload to boot), I have found myself flagging from time to time. These are real warning signs. And, as I have mentioned in another reflection, such an approach not only damages us personally but also impacts our loved ones as well, for we are unique and invaluable to them (albeit by no means indispensable as far as our own jobs are concerned, which is somewhat ironic).[27]

And the proof of the pudding, as they say, is in the eating – or should I say sleeping. When I have gotten quality amounts of sleep, I find that I not only function better, I actually *feel* healthier and more vibrant. The aim for me now is to be more *disciplined* and to try to get to bed earlier; to not be anxious about work and to also not get caught up with late night activities, including surfing the Internet. A *balance* is required, although it will be difficult, given the ingrained (bad) habits of many past decades (hence, the need for *discipline*). Indeed, viewed from a *broader* perspective, the concept of *balance* is indeed an integral part of *life* itself, that is to say, a balance between activity and rest (the latter requiring, of course, adequate sleep).

---

27 See Reflection 5: You are Indispensable to Your Family – Importance of Family.

I find it rather ironic that we have – especially in this day and age – to exercise *discipline* in order to *rest*! However, such rest is absolutely essential and we do ourselves, especially our minds and bodies, a terrible disservice (and, ultimately, even irreparable harm) by not exercising such discipline.

> ***Adequate sleep is not merely optional,***
> ***it is essential to our overall wellbeing.***

FINDING MEANING
IN LIFE

31

The Failure of 'Failure'

Yet Further Reflection on the Meaning of Success

We live in a materially driven society. This is evident right from when children are of school-going age. There is intense competition amongst children even before they have had an opportunity to experience true childhood. Naturally, adults are not spared either – it is a veritable rat race to what is hoped will be the top of the (material) ladder, with the accompanying mantra of "survival of the fittest". And so both children and adults alike are generally miserable and unhappy – even, most perversely perhaps, in the midst (in Singapore at least) of relative *material* prosperity for the most part.

However, the key premise underlying the notion of "success" as described briefly in the preceding paragraph is that of *material* success. What appears to have been neglected is success in the *non-*material sense – a life that is based on *values* such as happiness, integrity and honesty, as well as service and sacrifice.[28] The (again, material) sceptic would pour scorn on such values. Yet, without them, life as we know it becomes an empty and, frankly, arduous or even torturous experience on a perpetual treadmill until this physical life is over. Indeed, *this* type of success is, in my view, a *failure*, in fact, for several reasons.

---

28   See the reflections in the section entitled "Values and Disciplines".

The first reason is a simple one (albeit unpalatable in today's world). The failure to achieve material success in a given situation is *not necessarily* a disaster. On the *contrary*, it is only from our failures that we *learn* and, through learning, become wiser and therefore more *successful*. Indeed, many people may "fail" early on in life, only to find their true calling later (and become a success, perhaps even when measured by the material standards of the world). Hence the label "failure" that is coined by the world as we know it is – for this very reason – *itself* wrong and in a very fundamental sense a "*failure*" of both logic as well as aspiration. The fact of the matter is that people who are worldly and materialistic do not wish to admit that they are themselves imperfect and, as imperfect human beings (which we *all* are), will *themselves* have encountered failure in the world from time to time. However, their conceit will not permit them to admit to this and this leads, whether consciously or subconsciously, to an arrogance and pride which blinds them to what *true* "success" is – a point to which I shall return towards the end of this reflection. Indeed, *true* "failure" is simply giving up on oneself and not persevering any more. Viewed in this light, those who are *materially* successful but superciliously full of themselves are, in my respectful view, *true* "*failures*".

The second reason is one that I have already touched upon – that *material* success *alone* centres on *a single value*, namely, *material greed*. How that can be construed as being true "success" frankly eludes me – except to the select cabal who conspiratorially subscribe to this narrow (and *perverted*) view of "success". The fact of the matter is that there are *many other values* out there in the world, a few of which I have touched on already. For example, one may be materially poor and yet be rich in honesty and integrity. One may also, to take another example, be materially poor and yet serve others to the best of one's ability. And, to take yet another example, one may be materially poor and yet be content as well as happy – indeed, many families around the world are like that. In this last-mentioned regard, many families have *no choice* but to be materially poor – for example, those who live in war-torn countries. However, in such a situation, we have witnessed, time and again (and even under the greatest of adversity), the willingness to share what little one has with another.

And so you, dear reader, might quite validly ask me – what, then, is true "failure" and, correspondingly, true "success"? Might I respectfully suggest that so long as we learn from our failures in life and persevere without giving up, that is indeed true "success". And I might add that when we truly impact *other lives* for the *better* (and *not necessarily* only in *material* terms), that might well *also* be said to be true "success".

Failure is only truly failure when
we give up on ourselves.

32

The Limits of Reason and the Mystery of Life

Faith and Hope

There is often much despair and hopelessness in the world. This is perhaps not surprising in light of the many difficulties we face as well as the suffering and injustice that abound in the world around us. In previous reflections, I have emphasised the need for nevertheless preserving and for impacting lives around us for the better (even though we may not, in the very nature of things, be able to physically measure such impact). Much as I continue to truly believe in this approach towards life, I also realise that it is not an easy principle to practise. I would like to suggest that this is due to at least two reasons.

The first is related to a point I have already alluded to: that we cannot actually measure, in a tangible manner, the impact that we have on other people's lives. This difficulty is often coupled with another limitation on this side of eternity – the finite nature of our own physical lives and that it is just a matter of time before the days allotted to us finally run out. That is why perhaps many people choose simply to be selfish and attempt to obtain the maximum material benefits for themselves during their lives (whether it be in the form of material wealth and/or power and status) and abandon the ideal to which I have just referred.

There seems to me to be a second – and closely related – point that is often not even in the general consciousness of people. The dilemma that we find ourselves in stems from the fact that we are *only* using our *reason* to determine how we should live our lives. And the use only of reason leads, I believe, to much confusion. For example, although we desire to impact other people's lives for the better, we feel the countervailing tension to look after our own individual interests (especially since, as noted in the preceding paragraph, our physical lives are themselves limited in duration). This is nothing new and, indeed, has manifested itself even in the more abstract philosophical question as to whether it is possible to resolve the tension between the attainment of communitarian or societal goals on the one hand and the satisfaction of individual desires on the other (where there is no coincidence of interests) – a question to which there has still been no satisfactory philosophical answer.

I locate my own solution to this dilemma by way of a spiritual solution. However, I acknowledge that not everybody believes in a higher being and/or order of things. *Even then*, might I suggest that one possible way forward is to first *acknowledge the **limits** of reason*. This is not to state that reason is irrelevant, far from it – it is absolutely essential. However, when we face the intractable difficulties which I have outlined at the start of this reflection, it seems to me that we need to acknowledge that reason *alone* will not furnish us with a satisfactory solution because *life as we know it is too large and too mysterious to be tackled satisfactorily on the basis of reason alone*. On the contrary, the use of reason *alone* might be apt to confuse and even lead to unnecessary frustration, with the possible consequence that we actually lose hope. At this point, might I suggest further that we need to *trust* that, as we attempt to live our lives in such a manner as to impact other people's lives for the better, our lives *will* have *meaning and significance – even if* *we cannot rationalise it on a purely logical level (principally through physical measurement, as alluded to above).* I do admit that this requires a kind of "*faith*". That is where, speaking for myself, my *spiritual* beliefs *aid immeasurably in encouraging me that this "faith" I speak of is not a "blind" one that is wholly devoid of reason or logic.* Put simply, it is the *integration* of faith and reason.

However, *even if* one does not believe in a higher being and/ or order of things, I do truly believe that one should *still* exercise a kind of "*faith*" and attempt to live one's life to impact other people's lives for the better. I have the "*faith*" that, as one engages in such a practice, one will somehow *confirm* the *value* of it, even if it is not viewed in spiritual terms as such. More than that, it will, I also believe, create a "virtuous cycle" so that the more this is practised, the more one will be encouraged by *real hope* that will, in turn, encourage one to persevere. At this juncture, there is a simultaneous integration of *the "head" and the "heart"*. We often think of the "heart" as being purely subjective. However, when it is *integrated* with the "head" in the manner I have just outlined, it gives *real (and objective) hope* for the present as well as the future.

Although the use of reason is essential,
it has limits and one should therefore also
step out in "faith" (as well as reason)
to impact other lives for the better, so as to
give both ourselves and others hope for
the present as well as the future.

33

The Limits of Human Knowledge

Knowledge has always been highly prized and has become all the more so in modern society. Indeed, students are increasingly caught up in the rat race of pursuing paper qualifications. The stress that this brings has – for some – become intolerable. Ironically, though, knowledge has become increasingly detailed as well as specialised. There used to be a time – in the era of polymaths – when a highly intelligent person could know virtually everything there was to know across a wide variety of disciplines. This is no longer the case. Indeed, academic dons frequently specialise nowadays in what is a sub-set of their individual discipline. There is also far too much knowledge out there in the world today. However, one thing has not changed – knowledge does, on occasion, puff oneself up. I would nevertheless suggest that there is actually nothing to be proud of. On the contrary, the facts just mentioned mandate humility instead. To reiterate, there is too much knowledge spread over too many areas such that it is impossible to know even close to everything. As just mentioned, even specialists in their respective fields often do not know everything but, instead, specialise in very narrow areas of their respective disciplines. And I can testify to this, having spent almost a quarter of a century in legal academia.

I would like to take this one step further. There is a sense in which even the greatest human thinkers will not be able to come even remotely close to answers to the most basic questions of life. The great irony, in my view at least, is that these basic questions are not that difficult to discern and in fact straddle virtually every aspect of our human existence, thereby cutting across a diverse variety of disciplines. However, whilst they are relatively easy to discern and identify, they are impossible to resolve. In this regard, I would like to share a little from my own experience.

Even when I was a fledgling legal academic, I was interested in many other disciplines – for example, history, philosophy, political science, sociology and science. Although I specialised in the law (which, in traditional perception at least, is perceived as being very technical as well as narrow), I always had a sense that it was just one piece in the larger jigsaw puzzle of life. Indeed, it did not take long to realise that one could not really understand the law (especially the law "in action") without understanding how it operated in its wider milieu. This was, in fact, the premise that resulted in my doctoral thesis on the development of Singapore law. I began to read everything I could lay my hands on that had to do with Singapore itself. Fortunately, this was still possible decades ago as various writings on Singapore in the various disciplines were still relatively few in number. This is no longer the case.

Even then, I found relating the development of Singapore law to its broader historical as well as socio-economic and political context an enormously difficult task. Part of the problem was to locate a theoretical framework or a set of theoretical frameworks that could capture the myriad of details that numbered in their thousands (probably tens of thousands) and make sense of them. Absent a theoretical framework, I would have been lost in a sea of specific, yet seemingly unconnected, details. I attempted to work out this conundrum in a review essay and, subsequently, in the first chapter of my thesis. It vexed me greatly and I do not think that I located any satisfactory solution. Little was I to know that this was a problem that engaged the best of the Greek philosophers as well and is one that, in one form or another, is to be found in every discipline (whether it be in the law, in economics, in political science, or even in the discipline of science itself).

So that is one basic – or, more accurately, fundamental – problem of human knowledge, and centres on how one makes sense of specific details of life through theoretical frameworks (or models, or whatever terminology one prefers). It does not help that life is indeed "messy". It is a problem that is to be found even within a specialised discipline itself and the difficulties are multiplied in an exponential fashion when one seeks to translate it to other areas and, ultimately, the entire body of human knowledge. Just the thought of such an enterprise might be sufficient to blow one's mind. In my view, it is an impossible task – if nothing else, because in addition to all the difficulties that I have outlined in the briefest of fashions above, there is also the rather practical and very real problem that any one human mind is *itself* finite and limited (in more ways than one).

What does all this mean? It does mean that one has to be humble. No matter how gifted we are, we will never be able to truly solve the *fundamental* problems of life in general and of the human condition in particular. All we have are "snapshots" of "snapshots", so to speak – that is, if we are fortunate and are also at the top of our intellectual game to begin with. Indeed, the *true* path to knowledge begins – ironically and even paradoxically – when we admit that we will never truly know the ultimate answers and that all we can do is to humbly learn as well as to do our best in order to contribute what we can to the body of knowledge that we are involved in at any given point in time.

> *There are limits to human knowledge and the true path to knowledge begins with the humility to acknowledge that we can only learn and that all we can do is to then try our level best to contribute what we can to the body of knowledge that we are involved in at any given point in time.*

34

The Limits of Human Knowledge
Further Reflection

In the previous reflection, I emphasised the limits to human knowledge and stated that the true path to knowledge begins with humility – the humility to continue learning as well as the humility to contribute our level best to the body of knowledge we find ourselves involved in at any given point in time. I sought to illustrate this point by demonstrating how vital it is – *regardless* of the discipline one is in – to locate sound theoretical frameworks and how extremely difficult it is to do so. Indeed, when applied to the entire body of human knowledge, the task would be an impossible one.

In the present reflection, I would like to elaborate upon that illustration by locating it in the context of what I think is an utterly fundamental issue. I would venture to suggest that it is one that is to be found in relation to *every* area of human knowledge. In a nutshell, it relates to the problem of *relationships*. More specifically, it concerns the perennial problem of how *individuals* are to relate not only to other individuals but also to *community or society* as well. It is so fundamental that, as already mentioned, it occurs in every discipline. In the discipline of economics, for example, there is the perennial debate as to whether a free market system based on individual preferences is or is not preferable against a communitarian system. The analogue of this in the sphere of political science is to be located in the (also perennial) debate between a system of individual rights versus a system such as Communism. In the sphere of philosophy, we find the (again perennial) debate between theories based on individual rights on the one hand and (countervailing) theories such as utilitarianism on the other. In the law, some critical legal scholars have referred to a similar conundrum as "the fundamental contradiction" where individuals require community in order to subsist as well as affirm their individuality whilst simultaneously having their individuality being (at least potentially) threatened by that very same community.

There have been a myriad of theories in every discipline or area of learning that seek to locate a *balance* between the individual on the one hand and the community that he or she lives in on the other. However, *none* – to the best of my knowledge – is even close to being successful (in the sense that it is generally accepted by the vast majority of scholars, let alone by people generally). This is not surprising in the least. As I pointed out in the previous reflection, life is "messy". In addition, the human mind is itself finite and limited. Yet, the *practical* result is that there continues to be strife in the real world even as more theoretical ink is spilt on a problem that may, in the final analysis, be impossible to resolve based on human reasoning alone. Just as the number of books mount up on the bookshelves, they are outstripped only by the difficulties as well as suffering that we find in the real world. That does not mean, however, that we give up looking for solutions. However, such solutions as there might be might well have to be found at a much more limited, even piecemeal, level. And they will need to be located with an attitude of humility and (perhaps more importantly) service.

There is *another* sphere of human learning which was once thought to epitomise *objectivity* in human knowledge. This is the sphere of the sciences. However, as the frontiers of science have advanced – especially during the past century or so – we have found that there is in fact much that we do not know and that scientific knowledge, far from demonstrating a concrete objectivity, has become even fuzzier and more malleable (consider, for example, the developments in quantum mechanics).

In summary, the old adage that the more we learn, the less we know has never been more true even as (perhaps ironically) knowledge as a whole has advanced by leaps and bounds. Humility is therefore required as well as a willingness to think of solutions that will actually benefit real people rather than be fixated on abstract theories that may be intellectually stimulating but practically sterile.

There should be humility in the pursuit of knowledge that benefits real people in a practical way.

35

Looking Beyond Ourselves

If we are brutally honest with ourselves, we will acknowledge that much of our lives is driven by our egos as well as our own material desires for wealth and/or power. There is nothing wrong with acknowledging our individuality for that is what distinguishes us

from others. However, real problems arise when we focus solely, or even mainly, on ourselves to the exclusion of others (especially those who are in need).

Although comics were frowned upon as juvenile literature when I was a child, I must say that I enjoyed them very much. They were a kind of "movie", which one could replay by re-reading them. I recall one comic in particular – in brief summary, it was about a hero who was then the fastest draw. He lost a gunfight with a young upstart because he was ill with a high fever at the time. At the rematch, he naturally won and when the young man responded by saying that he (the hero) was still the fastest draw around, the hero uttered the following words that had an enormous impact on me even as an eight-year-old and which have stayed with me for decades since: "There's always somebody with a faster hand and a keener eye, just over the horizon … and sooner or later, we all meet him!".

The lesson to me then, as now, is clear: no matter how talented or skilled we think we are, there will always be someone better. There is therefore no need to get caught up with ourselves; put another way, perhaps humility is not even a choice! However, as I settled into my new job as a law lecturer upon graduation from law school, it occurred to me that I could take that principle one step further.

As a teacher, there are no huge material rewards on offer. Indeed, to me at least, one major reward was interacting with students and discussing not only the law but also life with them. And it soon occurred to me that an indicia of success in that particular profession was training one's students (in law and, hopefully, in life as well), and even hoping that some of them would be better than oneself. If that sounds counterintuitive, it is only because one is still obsessed with the premise that success only occurs when it belongs to oneself exclusively. However, viewed in another light, it is no less an exclusive success when the fruit of one's labour has resulted in equipping others and even more so if the latter become so well-equipped that they are better than oneself. I must confess that it was by no means a natural process to arrive at this conclusion. I, too, had to fight the natural inclination to desire personal honour and accolades for myself – and myself alone. However, the teaching context assisted in no small measure. I do confess that it can be even more difficult to look beyond ourselves and accept that helping others is best in most other contexts. But it is not impossible. And this leads to my next point.

I have long been influenced by the fact that personal honour and glory die with us – at least on this side of eternity. In my view, if we truly desire to have an impact that lives on after (and beyond) us – what I have often termed "a *living* legacy" – that will only be possible if we impact the lives of others for the better in the hope that they, too, will do the same, as well as in the further hope that the cascading effect, as it were, will continue for as long as it is possible. That requires, however, no small measure of "faith". I have placed the word "faith" in quotation marks because that word often has religious connotations. I truly believe, though, that, *regardless* of our religious beliefs, we can still impact other lives for the better if we are truly minded to do so. However, we still need "faith" in the sense that we may never truly know whether we have been successful or not,[29] but that does not make it any less the right thing to do. In a world where we are constantly being told that we must strive for individual success and where narcissism has never been more rampant, this will not be easy. However, I do truly hope that we can all take a step back and, with that fuller

---

29 See also Reflection 32: The Limits of Reason and the Mystery of Life – Faith and Hope.

and more holistic picture, endeavour to look beyond ourselves and help others wherever and whenever possible, particularly those who are in need.

We should always try to put aside our egos and material desires and try, wherever and whenever possible, to help others, particularly those in need.

36

Like Candles Burning Brightly
Living a Meaningful Life

In a previous reflection, I considered the need to persevere and not despair – to continue to live life as meaningfully as one can in an imperfect world that is full of injustice and suffering.[30] Indeed, apart from injustice and suffering, there is one ultimate "enemy" who can be "delayed" but who can never be avoided – physical

---

30 See Reflection 22: Do Not Despair, and Continue to Live Life Meaningfully – An Imperfect World.

death. This particular reflection, whilst merely underscoring the same lesson as in the previous reflection (and, indeed, yet another), drives home the point in literally graphic terms.

Recently, I was reminded of the imagery of a candle. It was whilst I was at a church service and a couple of persons came forward – one to state that we should burn brightly like candles for our faith and another stated that we should trim our wicks in order to burn more cleanly and brightly for our faith. I was also almost simultaneously reminded of a secular reference to the same imagery – the song, "Candle in the Wind" (which was written in honour of the late American actress, Marilyn Monroe, and made famous by the singer-songwriter, Elton John).

The song symbolises the fleetingness of physical life which, as I mentioned at the outset of this reflection, must ultimately follow, whether sooner or later, in physical death. It is like a candle in the wind which, come what may, will ultimately be snuffed out.

However, the former (of the candle burning brightly) seemed to me to be the more relevant and more inspiring imagery. Indeed, I was also reminded of the times as a child when we had the occasional blackouts. On these occasions, it was extremely inconvenient, to say the least. One had to operate in pitch darkness (which meant not being able, from a practical perspective, to operate at all). It was therefore such a relief when the candles were brought out and lit. It made such a difference! One could see where one was going and could at least operate in a minimal fashion until the electricity was restored. What I did notice, however, was the fact that, if a blackout lasted too long, the candle would melt completely down into a waxy mess and one would have to light yet another candle in order to provide the requisite light in the darkness.

Our lives are very much like candles. They are lit not just during blackouts; on the contrary, they are lit the moment we are born. And like the candles in blackouts and the song referred to earlier, these candles/lives have a limited duration whether we like it or not. *How* we burn and *where* we choose to place ourselves are therefore of crucial importance. With regard to the former, some of us are concerned, unfortunately, with burning the candle at both ends; put simply, the focus is not on bringing meaningful light to others but pushing, for example, to impress immediate bosses. The irony is that, by doing this, we are not only shortening the duration of the candle's use but also shining our light in an ultimately useless way – which brings me to the latter point. As already mentioned, where we choose to place ourselves is vitally important. It seems to me that we should place ourselves where we will assist the most people at any given point in time. The focus, in other words, is on bringing light and assistance to others as best we can. It also seems to me to be the most meaningful way of living one's (limited) life on this side of eternity. Indeed, it seems to me most meaningful *especially if* one does not believe in a life beyond this physical existence.

In what is basically a profoundly dark world, it is my hope that we will all live in such a manner as to impact other lives for the better whenever we can. May we bring light in the darkness and, as a result, comfort and strength to others.

Living a meaningful life in an imperfect world means impacting other lives for the better – like a candle shining in an otherwise dark place.

REFLECTIONS ON LIFE
IN A TIME OF PANDEMIC

37

Choose Life

I was hoping so much for the year 2020 to arrive. Somehow (perhaps superstitiously, I am ashamed to confess), I thought that my life would turn a corner for the better. The few years prior had been some of the most stressful I had ever faced in my life. Both my parents had been seriously ill and I lost both of them within a short space of some eight months. There were many other deaths of relatives and friends as well. Indeed, in the depths of my heart, I just felt that a dark hole of death had somehow opened up in the finite space of my life. Notwithstanding this, my work did not suffer (and here I have to say it must have been, from a personal perspective, only by the grace of God). Indeed, from one point of view, I had never been more productive in my working life. Yet, the stench of death, coming at all too regular intervals, rendered any achievement at work somewhat meaningless. The stress is also reflected in the fact that this is, in fact, my first new reflection in over a year.

And so 2020 came, and my family and I celebrated the wedding of my younger daughter. It was indeed an extremely joyous occasion and, for the first time in years, I felt the weight that had burdened my life lift a bit. However, this was not to last for very long, if at all. There were more deaths. And then, like a bolt from the blue, the COVID-19 pandemic struck not only Singapore but the rest of the world as well. As I write these words, this is the first day of a month-long stay-home measure implemented by the government to help curb the spread of the virus. Added to the stench of death I mentioned earlier is the stench of fear. Fortunately, my work has not been affected by telecommuting. Indeed, looked at from one point of view, my work productivity has even improved. However, this is little consolation as I write this reflection during my lunch break. The shadow of death now no longer resides around me – it is found globally. Even as I check at regular intervals, the number of confirmed cases of COVID-19 and, worse still, the death toll continues to rise at a rate that is both alarming as well as distressing. And this has prompted many thoughts and reflections.

The first – and perhaps most basic – is that life is precious and that is why the rising death toll has hit me so hard. I cannot even begin to imagine the almost infinite amount of grief that is being poured out around the globe constantly since the pandemic struck. This is because each death is not only a mere statistic – each death represents a tragedy of unspeakable proportions to the family which it touches. Having said that, I know that there are those who might feel that life is not worth living and that is understandable (albeit extremely unfortunate) as well. However, I believe that is the exception rather than the rule. Quite apart from the very *practical* fact that we need to have life in order to – well – live it, there is (as I have stated in previous reflections) a point to life, which is, to put it simply, to live our lives in a manner that will impact the lives of others in a meaningful way.

The present pandemic reminds us that life is not only fragile but that it is also immensely precious. And we must therefore never give up – even under such horrendous circumstances. Where there is life, there is always hope. However, we treasure our lives not as things in themselves for they would simply rot away on the inside if we adopt such a selfish attitude. On the contrary, we treasure our lives in order that we may then live our lives with meaning and purpose. Indeed, we can utilise this horrendous time to help others in whatever way we can. You might be surprised, but even the smallest of gestures could mean so much to someone who is currently in dire straits. May we continue to be wise in our activities in order to do our part in preserving life as well as bringing this pandemic to an end. May we also have a renewed appreciation for the preciousness of life and attempt our level best to help others in need during this time as well.

Life is precious, and where there is life,
there is always hope.

38

Wealth Cannot Buy Health

I recall mentioning to a few younger colleagues not so very long ago that although we were materially less well-off generally a generation ago, we were more content. Life nowadays, though, is quite different. Amongst the many changes that have since emerged is the pursuit of material wealth. From a personal perspective, what is even more troubling is the fact that many people are now of the view that material wealth is everything. Indeed, some go further and arrogantly "flaunt" their wealth. I have put the word "flaunt" in quotation marks because, on many occasions, such flaunting of wealth is sought to be masked in polite language and genteel conduct but is, in my view, still not something that is at all principled, let alone desirable.

The problem with the single-minded pursuit of material wealth is that it often warps one's value system. And when that is the general ethos, it leads to a society that tends to become less principled as a whole. The more serious problem is that when such an attitude becomes an integral part of the prevailing social culture, it becomes legitimised even though it is, in substance, unprincipled.

On a practical level, as the old adage goes, "Money cannot buy you happiness." Indeed, families have even been torn asunder as a result of quarrels over businesses and/or inheritances (as the many bitterly fought court cases will bear testimony to). During this difficult time we are experiencing as a result of the COVID-19 pandemic, one could go further and say, "Money cannot buy you health." That is indeed the reality. The COVID-19 virus is no respecter of persons, let alone the size of their bank accounts or wallets. And when it is contracted, no amount of money can *guarantee* recovery.

On another level, during this difficult time, the pursuit of material wealth necessarily takes a back seat, in any event, to the preservation of health and life. After all, of what use is material wealth when it is not accompanied by good health? Indeed, good health is a prerequisite to the pursuit of material wealth or any other aim for that matter. The present times are therefore not only worrying but are also sobering as well. They force us to reassess our priorities and to realise what is truly worthy and therefore truly worth pursuing in life. And, in my respectful view, whilst one has to find ways of earning a living (which is, after all, not only necessary but also the right thing to do), material wealth is not everything. Indeed, if one is honest with oneself, one does not have to be materially wealthy in order to live a comfortable life. Far from it. Often, the material wealth that is displayed is mere self-indulgence or even takes the form of arrogance when it is "flaunted". The fact of the matter is that wealth cannot buy you health – or, for that matter, many other things that are more worthwhile in life, for example, warm family ties as well as respect.

Wealth cannot buy you health or, indeed, most of what is worthwhile in life.

39

Worldly Status Cannot Guarantee Health

I have found over the years that there are at least two things which many persons pursue enthusiastically or even obsessively: material wealth and worldly status. This is, in fact, understandable if one takes life at a relatively superficial level. The crucial problem, in my view, is that after a while, such a superficial view, when accepted as the norm and practised in a widespread fashion, can take on a life and reality of its own. In the previous reflection, I wrote about the former; in the present, I write about the latter. In many ways, though (as I shall explain briefly below), both material wealth and worldly status often interact with each other.

The obsession with worldly status permeates every aspect of our lives and every strata of society. Indeed, I have noticed that this obsession is to be found within almost every cluster at the workplace – even within clusters in which one would not ordinarily expect such an attitude to be present (for example, administrative pools where the work concerned is relatively simple and straightforward or in academia where scholars are supposed to be focused on their research and teaching, to take but two, albeit otherwise quite contrasting, examples). Perhaps this is an endemic and negative part of the human condition – the need, even in (or perhaps especially in) the pettiest of situations when nothing is substantively at stake, to try to exert power and influence over others. This is, of course, the very antithesis of the humility I have written about in another reflection.[31] Not surprisingly, there is often, as alluded to above, the interaction of such an attitude with the pursuit of material wealth – for example, it has sometimes been said that "money is power", and there is unfortunately not a little truth in such a statement.

The problem with such an attitude is that it often develops insidiously, to the point where one can even rationalise it away and believe that one's attitude is justified, even though it is not possible to do so objectively. Indeed, true humility does not come easily or even naturally to most of us (myself included). One must always be conscious of the need to check oneself until true or real humility becomes almost second nature in one's life. This is truly not an easy road to travel. When I was a lecturer at the university, I would, on occasion, tell my students that my hope was that they would contribute much in positions of significance and authority in the future, but that my greatest worry was that they might get too caught up with their own selfish ambitions once they had attained positions of authority. As I have just mentioned (and I think that it bears repeating), to overcome this obstacle is easier said than done: the vanity and ego I have just alluded to are often insidious influences and self-rationalised.

However, one thing became remarkably clear during the COVID-19 pandemic – the COVID-19 virus is no respecter of persons. Even those of high worldly status have been struck by the virus. And, indeed, their worldly status was also no guarantee as to the duration of recovery, or even of recovery at all. This is a sobering thought indeed – and something for all of us, especially those who lord it over others by virtue of their worldly status, to think about.

---

31 See Reflection 13: Yesterday's Newspaper Headlines, Today's Fish and Chips Wrappers – Fame and Humility.

If I may digress somewhat, there is a more fundamental question – what is the point of achieving positions of worldly status and influence? Speaking for myself at least, there is really no point to it if it is merely to be achieved as a thing in and of itself because such an attitude will lead to corruption and rot within one's character and soul and/or may, even worse, lead to harm to others. However, when utilised wisely, one's worldly status can in fact be used to help others in need – for example, to ensure that things are done in the correct and principled way in order that others who are in need are in fact benefitted. However, this will not be easy. To those, however, who are wont to act otherwise, the present COVID-19 pandemic is a timely reminder that they are by no means invulnerable and that their worldly status counts for nothing except to the extent that they use it for the good of others.

Worldly status cannot guarantee you health or, indeed, most of what is worthwhile in life.

40

Rest, Reflect, Recalibrate

Much has been written about the COVID-19 pandemic. Indeed, most of the news nowadays seems to focus almost entirely upon it. This is not surprising since it has now come to dominate our lives – for the most part, unfortunately, in the context of fear. Many articles have attempted to locate silver linings during this extremely dark time. And a great many of those have pointed to the fact that the pandemic has forced us to stop and reflect. There is much truth in this. But the key question is – what is the point to this?

I think that the first point is that, for many of us, before we can even contemplate reflection, we need to rest. And the COVID-19 pandemic has in fact made most of us take an "enforced" rest. For now at least, my family and I are confined at home, permitted to leave only to obtain essential supplies. Yes, work goes on because, fortunately, the nature of my work permits virtually everything I need to do to be done in the confines of my home. However, I have also learnt the meaning of slowing down and have discovered, as I have written about in a separate reflection, that there is indeed too much unnecessary busyness in my life.[32] Such busywork is now no longer much evident. Somehow, the pandemic has forced everyone to be more focused. Indeed, even meetings conducted

---

32 See Reflection 27: The Meaninglessness of 'Busyness' – Yet Further Reflection on Work.

remotely have left little time and appetite for rambling or the desire to impress. Speaking personally, this is all to the good because we often sacrifice the crucial (for example, family) at the altar of self (for example, impressing the boss as well as others) and more's the pity when we do not even consciously realise we are doing so. And so the present situation has forced us to become more focused in thought and deed and, in the process, freed up time to *rest* as well.

And rest, as I have written about in yet another reflection, especially sleep, is vital.[33] For me at least, the extent to which I had in fact been sleep-deprived was driven home in no uncertain terms. Many of us are functioning almost on "auto-pilot" – indeed, we may well have numbed our bodies and minds, and conditioned them into functioning beyond reasonable expectations (probably damaging them in the process). However, with the present "enforced" rest, I would not be surprised if many of us have realised that this was not only unhealthy but also unnecessary.

With the "brakes" having been applied (albeit involuntarily) on our lives, many of us have, I believe, also been afforded the time to *reflect* on our lives, as well as the meaning of our lives. Whilst such reflection ought in fact to be the norm, at least from time to time, few of us actually find the time to do so. On the contrary, for many of us, time is just a blur, "gobbled up" by the busyness of – well – everything. Now that we have the time to reflect, I would not be at all surprised if many of us then take the opportunity to *recalibrate* our lives – to reassess the direction that our lives have taken thus far and where we want to go from here.

Amongst other things, we need to ask ourselves whether what we strive for is truly meaningful and whether the sacrifices we have had to make were worthwhile (and, if not, whether we would like to make adjustments, even radical ones, for the future). We need to ask ourselves what is truly meaningful in each of our lives

---

33 See Reflection 30: Rest for Life – Sleep.

and whether life as we have lived it thus far has either helped or hindered us from realising such meaning. We need to ask ourselves what we truly need – not only for physical sustenance but also for the deeper development of our souls as well. These are not easy questions to address – yet, they are vital questions which we must address. I suspect that many of us are afraid of having to address them directly, which is why the busyness we have been occupied with furnishes us with a convenient excuse not to do so. However, the COVID-19 pandemic has removed such an excuse, and that having been said, it may not be a bad thing after all.

We should pause periodically to rest, reflect and recalibrate our lives.

41

A Reminder on the Importance
of Family

Sometime back, I wrote a reflection, the point of which was to emphasise that whilst we are not indispensable at the workplace, we are indispensable to our respective families.[34] During this difficult time engendered by the COVID-19 pandemic, it is good to underscore this point. And it might be appropriate to begin with the observation (or, rather acknowledgment) that, in reality, virtually all families have internal problems and that this is so to a greater or lesser extent. My earlier reflection did not deal with this more sensitive as well as delicate point and I want to come back to it later in this reflection. However, let me commence on a more positive note and emphasise how important families are in helping each one of us to cope with the present crisis. Indeed, it is during times such as these that we learn to appreciate our families more. Many families have been brought closer together for there is nothing like such a crisis to focus our minds on our loved ones and their safety as well as health. Many of us will try to render help to our family members even if we are physically apart. Technology has, in fact, facilitated communication across physical distances and even nations. And for those with religious beliefs, prayer is another way in which we can care for our

---

34 See Reflection 5: You are Indispensable to Your Family – Importance of Family.

loved ones (especially when we are physically separated). Family members who are living with each other have utilised the time to bond with each other and such an opportunity is in fact quite precious given the busyness of both working life and even school. And, of course, family members have learnt to demonstrate extra care for each other at this difficult time.

However, what about families whose members, for whatever reason, do not get along? There is no easy answer to this question – not least because family problems can vary so very much and it is therefore difficult to generalise. However, even under such negative circumstances, perhaps this is the appropriate time to put aside one's differences. No matter what such differences might be, they would probably pale into insignificance in light of the dire situations across the globe. More importantly, such situations remind us that life is short and that the bitter root of anger, discord, hatred and regret is not really worth holding on to. On the contrary, by releasing such negative feelings, we simultaneously release the internal burdens within and free ourselves as a result, ridding our bodies and souls of the poison of toxic relationships. Indeed, familial relationships are organic and any injury that is inflicted will necessarily be felt not only by the ones on whom the injury is inflicted but also by the person who inflicted that very injury itself. Whether we like it or not, families were intended to be organic bodies that would exist harmoniously from within. Whilst this is not always the case, I hope that we will all take time to not only treasure existing family relationships but also try our level best to bring healing wherever possible where there are fractures and fissures within such relationships.

Family always matters.

42

An Opportunity to Show Kindness

I wrote a number of reflections, some time ago, all of which centred on the theme of realising meaning in our lives by helping others and by not underestimating the power of little kindnesses.[35] However, all this is theory – as with most things, *practising* this

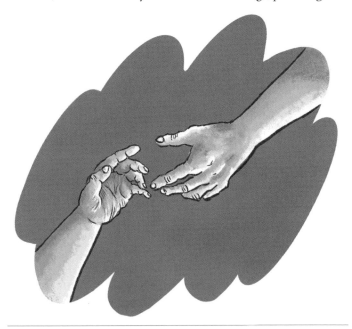

---

is easier said than done. Indeed, with the present COVID-19 pandemic, showing kindness may be particularly difficult since one may not be able to act from a position of comfort, let alone strength. Some may even argue that this is probably the worst time to show kindness since one has to look after oneself and one's family first. And we have seen more than shades of this in some of the hoarding, for example, that went on, at least during the initial stages of the outbreak.

Fortunately, however, the outbreak has also resulted in many acts of kindness as well, as the COVID-19 pandemic constitutes an ideal opportunity to show kindness to others. Quite obviously to begin with, there will be many more situations where persons are in need or even in distress and the opportunities for demonstrating kindness will increase manifold. During this difficult time, many of us will, I hope, realise that it is in fact quite liberating to live life simply and that, in the final analysis, we really do not need that much to not only survive but also be comfortable as well. If we can arrive at and internalise that realisation, we will then be afforded the opportunity to release our own resources to help others in need. The upshot of all this is that, much as we would wish that the COVID-19 pandemic never happened, the silver lining is that there are, in fact, many opportunities to show kindness to others in need as a result. And, as I have just mentioned, many of us do also, in fact, have the resources to show such kindness during this difficult time. And this has indeed been the case, judging from the numerous accounts of acts of kindness across the globe during this horrendous time.

Most importantly, perhaps, the concrete demonstration of such kindness often begins with the first "baby step". May all of us make that conscious effort to take that first step, if we have not done so already, to render an act of kindness to someone in need – even if it might not appear to be a very significant act. As I have mentioned, we cannot underestimate little acts of kindness. And may those first steps blossom into a natural and continuous flow of such acts which will contribute to a stream – and ultimately rivers – of kindness flowing within as well as across nations.

Adversity opens the door to acts of kindness, but we need to take the first concrete and practical steps to show kindness to others.

43

Wisdom and Technology

When I began my academic career approximately four decades ago, mechanical and electric typewriters as well as the fax machine were our mainstays. We had only just entered the age of affordable dry photocopying. Basic personal computers were still some years away. Legal research was still conducted manually, and each piece of research took an inordinate amount of time (and was subject to human error). Technology has since wholly transformed the way we work and, indeed, the way we live. Unfortunately, however, it is a double-edged sword. Whilst the Internet is a marvellous and extremely effective resource for all kinds of research or even everyday queries, it is also often the purveyor of gossip, rumours and fake news. The anonymity of the Internet coupled with various forms of social media also often result in exaggeration of biased views and even unwarranted abuse as well as cyber bullying. The Dark Web conceals all manner of unwholesome or even evil as well as profoundly harmful transactions. It is still very much the new "Wild West", so to speak.

And that is why we need wisdom in the use of technology. As with all things, the attitude as well as purpose with which a particular thing (here, technology) is used is all-important. If harnessed for legitimate purposes, technology can be a real boon: not only does it reduce the time taken to locate information but it also ensures that people will be able to communicate instantaneously – often across physical borders, thus bringing loved ones closer together (and often visually as well). In this last-mentioned regard, this is in sharp contrast to the time when I was studying in the USA many decades ago and had to restrict myself to ten-minute calls back home because each minute of telephone time cost so very much. Fast forward almost four decades and technology has become not only more useful but even virtually indispensable in a myriad of other ways. I have in mind, in particular, the COVID-19 pandemic. But for technology, everything would have come to a standstill with the onset of this terrible pandemic (which is still with us even as I write this reflection). Many meetings, classes and even court hearings are now conducted by Zoom.

On the other hand, we need wisdom to prevent *abuse* of technology in ways that have already been alluded to above. Given the nature of technology, the consequences of such abuse can be extremely devastating in both its reach as well as its harmful consequences for both individuals and institutions alike. Wise counsel from parents for the young and the wisdom to use technology only in ways that improve and/or edify from those of us who are older are therefore imperative. In this former regard, parents themselves must be role models by setting a good example whilst counselling their children on how to use technology wisely and to simultaneously avoid all the pitfalls and temptations as well as traps that are rife within it. This will require discipline by all concerned. This is because it is all too easy to succumb to our baser instincts and desires, which can take a myriad of forms. Indeed, due to the very nature of technology, any descent into darkness and despair can be both swift and steep. And the recent scams perpetrated against a major local bank resulting in innocent customers losing millions of dollars, constituting life savings for some, is a further – and grim – reminder of why wisdom in the use of technology, including vigilance and the implementation of relevant safeguards, is imperative.

It is my hope that all of us will harness technology only for good, whether in ensuring higher quality and productivity in our work or for reaching out, even across jurisdictions, to minister to others in need. And may we teach as well as counsel our children to be wise in the use of technology, not forgetting, of course, that technology can never replace personal relationships, although it can do much to enhance them.

We should always harness and
use technology wisely.

44

On Life and Death (1)
Time is Limited

There have been many – as well as many reminders of – life lessons during this extremely difficult time we have all had to undergo as the COVID-19 pandemic has generated much fear and paralysis across the globe. Even as I write these words, there is no tangible sign that the situation will abate in any significant manner. Put simply, life as we know it has probably been changed irrevocably.

Although the reflections in this book are intended to remind us of lessons as to how we should live our lives, the COVID-19 pandemic has not only made life more complicated but has also rendered my reflections increasingly "fuzzier" as there has been a realisation that the pandemic has forced me to think about *even more* fundamental issues – in particular, about the meaning of life and death itself. Most of my reflections thus far have operated on the assumption that we need not worry (excessively at least) about constant as well as fundamental threats to the very lives we possess. Indeed, even without such worries, it is not easy to live one's life meaningfully. However, the COVID-19 pandemic has taken the issue one fundamental – and visceral – step further: What is the meaning of life itself? This must surely be the fundamental assumption surrounding the immense despair that has arisen across the world as a result of the pandemic, in particular, the horrendous number of deaths that assail and, indeed, frighten us. Implicit in all this is, as I have pointed out in an earlier reflection, that life is precious.[36] However, just as life is precious, it is also *necessarily limited*. And it is this fundamental fact that I want to focus on in this reflection. I should also add that I took a long time to come to the starting-line for this topic because, as my future reflections will undoubtedly demonstrate, I really have no answers. And this, in turn, would mean that, unlike my earlier reflections, it may not be possible to summarise the lesson concerned pithily in a line or two (as I have done so far). But I have come to the point where I cannot justify avoiding the subject of life and death anymore, especially as the COVID-19 pandemic pounds us day after day. So let me begin with a more obvious point which simultaneously affords me a more gentle introduction into the topic at hand.

Time is limited. This is an undeniable fact of life. As the old saying goes, "Time and tide wait for nobody." What this means – whether we like it or not – is that our physical lives are finite. Put simply, our days are numbered, although we do not know when (and how) they will end. It is very natural, although I can speak only from my own experience, to take time (and our days) for granted when we are young. Indeed, when we are very young and are surrounded by a variety of rules and constraints, many of us wish that we could grow up faster so that we could live our lives more freely! And when we are young adults, many of us think that we have all the time in the world. In point of fact, this is quite deceptive, as I have discovered. And, of course, as we enter the autumn and winter of our lives (as I have), there is an acute realisation that time is extremely limited as we are nearer the end of our physical lives than the beginning. I believe that what the COVID-19 pandemic has done is to remind us in a very acute fashion that time and life is indeed limited. It has also reminded

---

36 See Reflection 37: Choose Life.

us – again, in a very acute fashion – that life is very uncertain and could (especially during these times) be abruptly cut short. This is a stark reminder and also a stark reality, and a fact we need to acknowledge in the first place before we can even begin to reflect on the meaning of life and death itself.

The number of our physical days is limited.

45

On Life and Death (2)

Life is Precious

I concluded my previous reflection in this final section (which stems from the COVID-19 pandemic) with the obvious yet fundamentally important point that the number of our physical days is limited. This is the case even for persons who are ostensibly

healthy. All physical life will ultimately end. It is only a matter of when it ends in fact.

What the COVID-19 pandemic has done has been to *underscore* the fact that physical life is limited and is not something that we can take for granted. Given that, as a result of this pandemic, our physical lives are not only at risk but could even be lost at any time engenders (for me at least) many questions as well as reflections.

In the meantime, I have returned to re-reading two books in which the respective authors dealt with the *certainty of impending* physical death (both had been diagnosed with terminal cancer and have since passed away). One author was a gifted surgeon (who was also gifted in literature as well, a complete and very rare "left-brain/right-brain" person).[37] The other was a gifted professor, teacher and scholar in computer science.[38] Both books are not only written clearly and excellently but also chronicle the deep feelings as well as struggles the respective authors and their families faced as they battled cancer. Perhaps most importantly, both authors also dealt with the existential question of physical death and the lessons that can be drawn for life. It is impossible to summarise these excellent books within the confines of this series of reflections; nor, in my view, would it be appropriate to do so. The books were intended to be *read* and then reflected upon, and I would therefore commend them to you in the highest possible terms. What I will state, however, is that both these books raise a number of very relevant questions, particularly in light of the COVID-19 pandemic and the fact that, as mentioned, our physical lives could not only be compromised but could even be lost in the blink of an eye.

One question – which seems so very basic – is this: Why is life so precious? (This is something I had, in fact, *assumed* at the start of this particular section of reflections.) Before I attempt to answer

---

37 See Paul Kalanithi, *When Breath Becomes Air* (Random House, 2016).
38 See Randy Pausch, *The Last Lecture* (Hodder & Stoughton, 2008).

this question, I know that there are many who are in despair and, very sadly, some have even taken their own lives. I do not pretend to know the answer. All I can say is that life is precious and that, where there is life, there is hope. For the vast majority of people, including the authors of the books I have just referred to, life is indeed precious. And this is often the case for a number of reasons.

The first and most basic reason is that, from a purely *practical* perspective, without life, we *cease* to *exist*. Correlatively, if we want to function as human beings, then we *need* to be *alive* in the first place. However, might I suggest that one of these functions also simultaneously confers much *meaning to life* – that being alive enables us to not only *form relationships* but *also* to *enjoy* those relationships. That is why it is often said that it is the person(s) who are left behind after someone passes away who feel the most grief. And that is why the authors of the books I have referred to above fought as hard as they could to combat their illness and to stay alive for as long as they could, whilst enjoying whatever remaining time that they had with their loved ones. This also reminds us that we should be glad to be alive and that we should treasure our relationships with our loved ones and friends.

> *Life is precious, not least because it enables*
> *us to form as well as enjoy relationships.*

46

On Life and Death (3)
Uncertainty and Randomness of Life?

The previous reflection in this section concluded with the point that life is precious, not least because it enables us to form as well as enjoy relationships. However, that being the case, the further question arises as to why the duration as well as quality of our lives are so uncertain – and whether, in turn, this is unjust and unfair. As we have seen in the two books I referred to in the previous reflection, terminal diseases such as cancer can strike with no warning whatsoever. A person could die suddenly of a heart attack, even if he or she is of a young age and not expected to do so. A person going for an evening stroll could suddenly be mowed down by a car that has gone out of control. The fact of the matter is that life is extremely uncertain, if we stop and truly reflect on it. The COVID-19 pandemic has merely *underscored* this uncertainty. Is life just a matter of random events? Was Shakespeare correct in *King Lear*, in observing that "[a]s flies to wanton boys are we to the gods. They kill us for their sport." Some would go further and argue that there is no such thing as a "God" (let alone "gods") and we are mere random products leading random lives.

I want to pause at this juncture to say that, throughout not only this section of "mini reflections" prompted by the COVID-19 pandemic but also throughout this entire collection of reflections as a whole, I have thus far avoided any mention (let alone discussion) of God. I had intended this section of reflections to be reflections which everyone (regardless of ethnicity, nationality, culture or religion) can engage with. However, when we discuss matters of life and death, it is very difficult to ignore completely the very large elephant in a very small room: ***the concept of God***. Indeed, ***how we approach*** matters of life and death in general and the perilous situation engendered by the COVID-19 situation in particular will, I suggest, depend very much on whether or not we believe in God and, if so, *which* God. Let me try to elaborate, taking things step by step (indeed, at this point, I have but only a very tentative next step).

Looking at things in the round, it seems to me that if one does not believe in the existence of God, then the randomness of life does make sense, albeit only in a manner of speaking. Why do I say that? It seems to me that an absence of belief in God does not necessarily solve the deepest problems that we all face. In the first place, it would mean that the physical life we are living is all that we have and that once we pass away physically, that is literally the end of the matter. This does not, of course, necessarily mean that life has no meaning at all (at least whilst it exists on the physical plane), but it does render the possible objective points of reference (especially of a moral nature) rather murky (a point I will return to at the end of this reflection).

More importantly, perhaps, such an approach does not admit of the best result because, as just mentioned, everything ends on physical death. Relationships formed earlier and felt to be extremely precious are not just severed by but are absolutely shattered into little pieces when physical death occurs. And that seems to me to be the reason why people who do not believe in the existence of God (and, by extension, the possibility, at least, of an afterlife) often advocate that life as we know it ought to be lived to the fullest for every moment is indeed precious as there is literally nothing else to look forward to when physical life ends. The COVID-19 pandemic merely emphasises this in no uncertain terms. Such an approach might also mean that it is futile to ask why there appears to be so very much randomness as well as injustice in the way life is in general and, in particular, why the pandemic does not otherwise appear to make much sense (in the way that life is taken even when it does not appear just or fair in the circumstances it has occurred).

However, I would respectfully suggest that such a rationalisation does not really work. It is only skin-deep as it necessarily begs the question as to why this is an issue or question in the first place. As importantly, such an approach *must necessarily presuppose an absolute value system* to begin with – that is to say, an absolute value system which is premised on mere physical human existence as a random fact, with no further existence (or at least the hope of it) beyond this *physical* life. That having been said, it is, nevertheless, *one* possible way of viewing life. Speaking personally, however, I think that it is a rather impoverished view that does not give that much hope and inspiration in the final analysis. To those who would argue otherwise and point to the possibility that one can nonetheless live one's life nobly in the service of others, I would respond and say that while this is all good, it nevertheless leaves unanswered one fundamental question: *how does one ascertain whether one's actions are "noble" in the first place when life is **assumed** to be **random**? Put simply, what is the **source** of "nobility" or any other value for that matter? Even more fundamentally, is the **very concept** of a "**value**" (such as "nobility") possible in a worldview which perceives life as being **merely** "material" or "physical" in a **random** universe? And yet (as I have just pointed out), such a worldview is **itself** an absolute value (albeit not one that gives that much hope). Is there an alternative?*

That is what I will begin to consider in the next reflection – while, at all times and in all fairness, bearing in mind the present approach as well.

> *Whilst the view that our physical*
> *life is all that exists is one way to*
> *perceive and live one's life, it leaves*
> *many questions unanswered and*
> *completely excludes any hope beyond*
> *physical death.*

47

On Life and Death (4)
Creation of Life

In the previous reflection, I suggested that whilst a view that the physical life we have is all that exists is one way to perceive and live one's life, it leaves many questions unanswered and completely excludes any hope beyond physical death. My own personal view is that there *is* a life (or existence) *beyond* physical death. I realise that the use of the word "personal" is a double-edged sword. However, what I would say is that I hope to demonstrate that such a "personal" view is not a wholly subjective and arbitrary one. I hope to take the reader through my own journey and try to show how objective logic as well as analysis dovetailed with my own personal experience. I should add that even those on the other side of the fence must concede that discourse through language is perfectly acceptable. Indeed, in the world as we know it, it is not only a means of communication with each other but is also the means through which we make sense of the world on a personal level.

I would like to commence my journey by looking at the world itself – first by looking at my own physical body. It is not simply a mass (or mess) of bones, flesh and blood. It is a complex organic whole which helps to generate thoughts and ideas and which (hopefully) interacts with and ministers to others as well.

However, on closer scientific examination, our very physical bodies are astonishing in their complexity and makeup (even within each organ itself such as the eye). To believe that all this was a random outcome – that life itself was a pure accident – is virtually impossible if we have regard to the laws of probability. I have often thought that there is an even more basic problem: How did the material from which we were "accidentally" formed, sometimes referred to as a primeval "organic or prebiotic soup", come into being in the first place? Indeed, this prompts a further question because the *existence* of such material *presupposes* not only the concept but also the *existence of both space and time*. However, that raises further – and perhaps even more fundamental – questions: *Where* did space and time come from in the first place? I have been speaking of our physical bodies. However, looking *outwards* and to *the world and nature (not to mention the universe)* themselves, it is, in my view, difficult to believe that what we see is all the product of mere chance. The astute reader would have realised by now that I have moved very close to a question I posed in the course of the previous reflection – *the concept of* **God**.

However, before proceeding to consider the concept of God, there is a related matter that needs to be dealt with, albeit in the briefest of terms. Much has been written about the topic of *evolution*. In a sense, I have already run ahead by alluding to the question of origins as well as the complexity of the human body. Traditional Darwinian evolution by way of natural selection proceeds, of course, from apes – in short, that human beings evolved from apes. While nobody disputes *micro*evolution (which can take place *within* a particular species), the *macro*evolution that is the foundation of Darwinian evolutionary theory is really devoid of any solid scientific evidence. For the purposes of the claims it makes, the fossil evidence is virtually non-existent, a weakness in his theory which even Darwin himself acknowledged.

Even the attempt at salvaging evolution by recourse to the theory of "punctuated equilibrium" (the argument that evolution was not a gradual process as such but, rather, that life evolved, as it were, in sudden bursts) is wholly unconvincing. More to the point, such an attempt to "save" evolutionary theory also raises the following poignant question: Does not the theory of "punctuated equilibrium" look, in the final analysis, very much like *creationism* (by God), particularly as both are equally unsupported by the fossil evidence? However, there is one difference – creationism, by definition, does not require any fossil evidence since *God* creates without (necessarily at least) the need for an evolutionary process. I realise, of course, that what I have said is only my personal view (that may or may not be shared even by other Christians). However, these are matters that, on a personal level, strengthen my belief that God exists.

I would like to end with this thought: If we are all the random products of chance, then there is *no basis whatsoever* for trusting in our own reason, let alone absolute moral values that are supposed to be discerned by our faculty of reason. I want to go a step further and argue that we are not only *not* the random products of chance but are the products of *a Creator – God*.

> **There is no chance that we are the random products of chance.**

48

On Life and Death (5)

Existence of God

I argued in the previous reflection that the theory of evolution is *itself* a *philosophy* or *metaphysical theory* which is unsupported by the very scientific methods that it claims underpin it. On the contrary, it is in fact everything that it accuses other theories, including creationism, of being – that such other theories are based on preference and value but are without empirical proof. What I would like to do now is to consider the argument that we are not only *not* the random products of chance (as the theory of evolution argues) but are, instead, the products of *a Creator – God*.

I do realise that, at this juncture, I am entering not only contestable territory but at least potentially controversial territory as well. This is especially so during present times when post-modernism has also come to the fore as a philosophy of life. Indeed, of all the reflections in this book, this is probably the most controversial. However, as I have emphasised in a previous reflection in this section of "mini reflections", in discussing matters of life and death, it is very difficult to ignore completely the concept of God and that how we approach matters of life and death will depend very much on whether we believe in God and, if so, *which* God.

Returning to the issue of whether God exists, in my view at least, there are a number of reasons as to why this is indeed the case. First, absent a transcendent argument with its source resting in God, there is no real answer to the especially moral and value-laden issues of life. One scholar, Professor Arthur Leff, put it well (although he fell short of actually stating that the *ultimate* "Evaluator" is, in fact, God):[39]

> Or to put it another way, one more congenial, I think, to both of us, by dispensing with God we did more than just free ourselves of some intellectual anachronism. We also dispensed with the only intellectually respectable answer to the ultimate "Why is it right to do X?" It was not so very long ago that most people (and I, too) could and did answer: "It is right to do X because God says so." That answer was at least intelligible, the only one that did not depend upon mere sublunary assertion, the only that even if it too involved the transformation of fact into value, was not for that reason insufficient. For assuming that God existed, and had commands, it was *He* who was evaluating our actions. He was not part of our evaluation system, nor were his evaluations subject, or even amenable, to our evaluations of *them*.

Secondly, there is the cosmological argument that, simply put, assumes that the universe, as an existing entity, had a cause – a first cause which cannot itself be explained, as infinite regress is not a reasonable option. This is, of course, consistent with what

---

39 See Arthur Allen Leff, "Book Review" (1977) 29 *Stanford Law Review* 379 at 888 (emphasis in the original text), reviewing Roberto Mangabeira Unger, *Knowledge and Politics* (The Free Press, 1975).

is essentially still the most widely accepted *scientific* theory today (popularly and perhaps crudely referred to as the "Big Bang model" of the universe). The elements of space and time are of crucial significance here. Indeed, the argument from infinite regress just referred to is implausible because, simply put, in order for the present moment to exist, it must have had a beginning; even more simply put, it is impossible for the present moment to have arrived *unless* it had somehow crossed or traversed an "actual infinite", which is, of course, a contradiction in terms. In addition, Professor Stephen Hawking's argument that the universe has no boundary and, hence, there is no edge of space-time relies, with respect, on imaginary numbers and many metaphysical assumptions.

Thirdly, there is the argument from design which has received even more striking and eminently solid scientific support from writers such as Dr William A Dembski (in the context of a theory of information) and Michael Behe (in the context of biochemistry). Briefly and simply put, this argument, first popularised by William Paley, points to such complexity and purpose in the world that one cannot but reasonably conclude that the world must have been created by a Designer God.

However, as I have alluded to above, even if one believes in the existence of God, the next question is this: *Which* God should we to believe in? This is the subject for a separate volume (indeed, *several* separate volumes) and I do not propose, in the context of the present book, to consider it, save to state what *I* believe in (which I hope readers would be at least mildly interested in). I believe in the Christian God. My own spiritual journey is a story in itself, culminating in my embrace of the Christian faith in my late 20s. It was by no means an intellectual assent, although now looking back over many decades, it was probably a mix of both intellect and experience (whose relationship is itself an extremely philosophical issue, amongst other things). As far as the intellect is concerned, I was later to discover its ballast in what we term collectively "Christian apologetics" which, for me at least, included historical as well as rational reasons supporting the death and, more importantly, the resurrection of Jesus Christ, reasons and records that support the reliability and veracity of the Bible, as well as arguments centring on the Trinity and especially the Holy Spirit (including, from an experiential perspective, my personal encounter with the latter throughout my Christian life). That having been said, like myself, each person must embark on his or her own personal journey to find God if he or she is indeed minded to do so.

I would like to conclude by exhorting you, dear reader, to seriously consider the argument that there is a God out there who gives meaning and purpose to your life. That, in turn, engenders hope and, hopefully, a love for others that translates into concrete action, which is so needful, especially during this continued COVID-19 pandemic.

There are sound arguments for the existence of God and, consequently, for us to seek meaning and purpose in each of our lives.

About the Author

Andrew Phang spent almost a quarter of a century in legal academia before joining the Supreme Court of Singapore as a Judicial Commissioner, Judge and then Justice of the Court of Appeal. He recently retired and is presently a Senior Judge as well as Distinguished Term Professor at the Yong Pung How School of Law, Simgapore Management University.

About the Illustrator

Christine Phang, the author's younger daughter, graduated Phi Beta Kappa from Carnegie Mellon University with a Bachelors of Humanities and Arts, majoring in Fine Art and Psychology. She is presently working as an art therapist at a community mental health clinic in California and has recently completed her Masters in Marriage and Family Therapy at Dominican University of California.

The author with his daughter, Christine.